The Freedom Revolution

Shift your business to another dimension
Break the business shackles and join the revolution

What's the best that can happen?

Penina Shepherd

Gratitude

I am grateful to you Dee Blick for being there for me, literally from day one.
You were my mentor, editor, marketing advisor, sounding board, rock and a friend.
You made the writing process so enjoyable and were always very professional.
It wouldn't have been the same without you.

I am grateful to you my dear colleagues at *Acumen Business law* for constantly inspiring and challenging me.
For being amazing colleagues to work with.
For always being so very Acusplendid.

I am grateful to you Jack Hubbard for lighting the match to write this book.
Just like that. As you do.

I am grateful to Ima, Osnat and Niso for believing in me.

I am grateful to you my Eden, Amelia and Zoe for being the reason for everything.

This book is dedicated to you Simon.
I am eternally grateful.
For everything.

Contents

"The way Penina has written this book is as though she had sat in front of me and poured her heart out on what it 'should be' and 'is' to be an entrepreneur today.

As an entrepreneur I wholeheartedly agree with her views of the modern revolutionary entrepreneur and that if we put people first, profit will follow. If we put our dreams first our fears will fade into a distant second place. Penina tells of a new modern business person that delivers results based on the old fashioned idea that if we care and believe in ourselves and put others first we can have success and I agree with her 100%.

Every person caught up in a corporate straitjacket must read this book. If you take Penina's words to heart I'm convinced you will not only agree with her but will breathe a huge sigh of relief that corporate is not the modern route. You'll be encouraged that you can achieve your dreams and make money without putting profit first."

Kevin Byrne
Entrepreneur & Founder of Checkatrade and Checkaprofessional

Your Journey, Yours and Mine

You are about to embark on a journey, the journey to freedom. So please make sure you don't fasten your seatbelt, you move about both during takeoff and landing and you don't simply wish for a safe journey, but an epic one too!

Just before you set off, can I make a small request? Can I join you?

Will you share your Freedom Revolution journey with me? You can share as little or as much as you wish. I love business stories and I really want to hear yours! Whatever stage you are at, whether you are starting out in business, are an established business person, a changemaker, a business student or you're thinking about going into business- I would love to hear your experience and your business story.

Please share your journey whilst reading my book. Has a particular chapter, paragraph, line or even a few words inspired you? Maybe you can offer your insights into how a certain part resonated with you the most, touched your core and why.

So please do get in touch with me via Twitter **@Penina_Shepherd** or my website on **www.penina.biz.**

Once you have finished the book and if you have had a positive experience perhaps you could spare a minute or two and write a review on Amazon? It's the virtual equivalent of a little 'pat on the back', and we all need that sometimes don't we...

I very much look forward to hearing from you.

Best
Penina

Whatever You Are Expecting it to Be, it Won't Be That

t will be so much better

There is a revolution happening around us in the business world. It has been happening slowly and most of us haven't even noticed.

Those at the forefront of the revolution not only do extremely well in business, but they also seem to be sailing through it in a state of bliss. This is true both for people setting up their own businesses as well as those who are high flyers in existing businesses.

If you want to fly high in business in this freedom era, you have to relinquish all the business preconceptions that weigh you down and join in. This book will explain how to do just that. There is still time for you to join the revolution and transform your business and career.

Think of what businesses looked like in the late 90s and in the first years of the new millennium and you will see a striking change. The attitude when setting up in business was: why make money for someone else when you can make that money for yourself? Building a career was all about climbing the 'corporate ladder' which was all about obtaining higher status and pay. Both businesses and top careers were seen primarily as a means of making money.

And then there was a coup.

In the revolution era there was a coup whereby money, the reigning king, was overthrown and replaced by something else. This book will show how in the revolution making money in business is a given but it is no longer the aim and how, precisely because of this, businesses in the revolution enjoy extraordinary financial success. Making money is an outcome achieved along the way, a very important one too, but it is no longer the driver, no longer the goal or the purpose.

Change is also apparent in the way we perceive business people in the business world. Before the revolution, it used to be that it was only the business founders that were highly regarded, but in the revolution era changemakers within existing businesses are taking the business world by storm.

Also it used to be that the term 'entrepreneur' was used only in relation to founders of large multi-million pound global corporations. Since the revolution, you see small business owners being referred to as 'entrepreneurs' and winning awards such as 'Entrepreneur of the Year' by various established organisations, myself being one such person. I was crowned by the British Chamber of Commerce as 'Entrepreneur of the Year for London & the South' and I certainly wasn't the founder of a multi-million global corporation. I was a corporate lawyer who had founded an innovative business law firm.

The revolution also changed our perception as to the type of businesses we regard as successful. Here too, it used to be primarily the large multi-million pound businesses that were regarded as successful. Not anymore. In the revolution, regional and smaller businesses also stand out as great successes in the eyes of business establishments, despite them not having the multi-million qualification criteria. The Financial Times listed my firm, **ACUMEN** BUSINESS LAW, in the Top 50 Groundbreaking & Innovative Law Firms in the whole of the UK & Europe, up there with the top magic circle

City law firms with international offices and hundreds of employees. It therefore seems that 'multi-million' status is no longer the sole criteria for measuring success in the revolution.'

Success, in the revolution era, is no longer just about money.

So how did this change become possible? It became possible thanks to the changemakers who came on the scene and revolutionised the rules of the business game, creating new business scenery. People in business are now no longer people driven by the pursuit of profit and nothing else, or obsessed with climbing up an invisible corporate ladder, with heads buried solely in spreadsheets and pay checks.

Business people in the revolution use their business and career as an extension of themselves to create something meaningful. They are changemakers and they are doing astonishingly well in this revolution. They are people who follow their dream and do something remarkable. Literally, something that is worth remarking on, and they are very successful. They are breaking the business shackles, ridding themselves of all the preconceptions and enjoying the freedom; freedom to pursue their passion, their dream, purpose and to be happy.

Great financial success is not the only natural outcome they enjoy from being free. Almost by chance, or so it seems, a business community is created around them operating as their 'groupies'. The groupies are their sales force, and they do it of their own accord because they want to join the revolution and spread its message.

'Changemaking happens when people fall in love with a different version of the future'.[1] (Seth Godin). Now more people than ever are falling in love with a new and different version of their business future. They all want to enjoy success in their business combined with that elated sense of freedom. Now more than ever is the time to set yourself free and join the revolution!

Whatever you are expecting that sense of freedom to be, however you think it will feel it won't be that.

It is going to be so much better.

Part I

Dream on!

*"As soon as you start to pursue a dream,
your life wakes up and everything has a meaning."*

Barbara Sher

Chapter I
Entreprewhores

The search
'If money was no object I would...' How would you complete this sentence? What would you do if money was no object in your business or career?

I was a corporate lawyer working in a top 100 law firm, when I asked myself that question. I was earning a very good salary and was climbing the corporate ladder with confidence. I was a Partner (the dream of every lawyer) and Head of Department (equally exciting) and was doing pretty well. I had two young children at the time (now three) and was endeavouring to make sure I had a good 'life/work balance' and that business and pleasure were kept well apart. I successfully followed all the good career rules.

But something was missing.

I was going through the motions and doing well, but I wasn't truly happy. My feelings would have been best described as 'satisfied', maybe even 'proud' to successfully follow a plan, but I didn't feel truly happy in my job. In pursuit of this missing piece of the jigsaw, I kept moving jobs hoping to find it at the next appointment. And even though I made progress from one job to another in terms of salary and status, that 'thing' I was looking for just wasn't there.

It seems I was not the only one experiencing this. According to the US Bureau of Labour Statistics, the average number of years that employees stay with one employer is 4.6 years. So there are many other people like me regularly jumping ship looking for something better.

But what became apparent in the revolution was that we were all looking for the wrong thing, therefore it is no wonder we couldn't find it; evidently, otherwise we wouldn't keep moving jobs every 4.6 years.

The top reasons employees stay in their jobs, according to the American Psychological Association, are 'I enjoy the work I do' and the job 'fits well with the other areas of my life'. Not salary (that came fourth), level of bonus, job title, status nor is it benefits like company car, pension and the like. It is about enjoyment and the way the job integrates in people's lives.

It seems to be about something other than money.

Entrepre...?
Before the revolution careers and businesses were primarily about making more money. I remember people used to say to me that I was quite entrepreneurial as I was climbing up the corporate ladder, gaining higher status and higher pay. But was I being entrepreneurial?

The Google definition of an 'entrepreneur' is:
"A person who sets up a business or businesses, taking on financial risks in the hope of profit."

The sole hope for you in business as an entrepreneur, according to this definition, is profit. So I can see why people thought I was being entrepreneurial when I was constantly pursuing higher pay as I was progressing in my career from one job to another.

But does this actually define an entrepreneur? I don't think it does and I don't think I was being entrepreneurial. Not at all.

In fact I believe I was being an entreprewhore.

I define an entreprewhore as:
> "A person in business who has given up on their freedom to follow their dream and is selling themselves short by being in constant pursuit of more profit and nothing more."

That was me, climbing my corporate ladder fully focused on making more money with complete disregard to my dreams, passion and core values. Giving up on my freedom and selling myself short by being in constant pursuit of higher status and higher pay and nothing more. And if that's you then like me you're missing an opportunity and no real entrepreneur likes that.

Money is present alright
This isn't saying that entrepreneurs and changemakers in the revolution shouldn't or don't make money, quite the opposite! Business people in the revolution era care about making money, they want to make money and are making money. They are doing extremely well financially. However there is one main difference.

Making money in the revolution is not the aim, the goal or the drive. Making money is a desirable outcome. An important outcome, but no longer the aspiration of business people in the revolution.

Trapped
Because you see, if making money is your only 'hope', to mention the term used in the Google definition of an entrepreneur, then you will never be truly free.

Think of those people who keep leaving their jobs every 4.6 years. They also make more money as they move from one job to the next, but what kind of lives do they live? Their lives are constantly on hold until the next job in 4.6 years' time where everything will be better and of course it rarely is, certainly not for the long term. They are not free; they are trapped in the infamous 'rat race', and I challenge you to show me one truly happy 'rat racer'.

This is true not just in relation to business people in careers, but also to business owners outside the revolution. They also make money, but they are equally trapped in the rat race. Constantly chasing the next big deal, endlessly embroiled in negotiations to squeeze the suppliers' margin as low as they possibly can, trying to get away with paying their staff as little as possible, all so they can make more money. They are not free either. They are also trapped. It is no surprise so many are just waiting to be bought out wondering when 'all this hassle' will end.

The thing is, before the revolution we were all entreprewhores.

Chapter 2
FREE Entrepreneurs

Pre-revolution evolution

A pre-revolution evolution has been taking place over the past ten to fifteen years in relation to multiple aspects of our lives including food, health, well-being, spirituality, and the environment as well as business. We started to pay more attention and make educated decisions with regard to these issues. In the new millennium we have seen a widespread transformation in our relationships with these facets of our lives and it has almost gone unnoticed.

For example, before the new millennium, veganism was regarded as an odd philosophy practiced by some hippy tribes. Today, it is nothing out of the ordinary. *"The Mintel Meat-Free Foods UK Report for 2012 shows that... meat-free sales set to reach £607m and... Almost four in 10 (38%) Britons have bought vegetarian or meat-free food, while one in five (20%) has bought free-from food."*[2]

Many more of us are only eating organic food as, according to a recently published TechSci Research report, *"Consumers across the globe are becoming increasingly health conscious..."* The research then points out that the *"global organic food market is projected to register a CAGR (Compound Annual Growth Rate) of over 16% during 2015-2020. Growth in the market can be attributed to... increasing awareness with regard to health..."*[3]

When it comes to spirituality, there has also been a tremendous awakening in the last decade. It has been said that in Brighton, my home town, it is easier to get your aura cleansed than your boiler fixed. Gustavo Tanaka, Brazilian author and entrepreneur, asks: *"How many friends do you have who practice yoga? What about meditation? Now think back, 10 years ago, how many people did you know by then who practiced these activities? Spirituality, for too long, was for esoteric folks, those weird-like and mystic people. But fortunately, this is also changing."*[4]

The same is correct with regard to the environment: *"UK increased recycling rates fastest in Europe over past decade... Although the UK started from a low base in 2001 – recycling rates were just 12% for all municipal waste – it increased by the greatest amount by 2010, reaching 39%, on a par with the average for the EU."* (The Guardian)[5]

As you can see, in the pre-revolution evolution there was a mammoth change affecting all aspects of our lives whereby considerations other than money were of significance to us in everything we did. This change hasn't skipped the business world, quite the opposite. It created a movement in the business world too. It manifested in a revolution of business people seeking to be free of the old business ways, breaking down the shackles and starting to see things differently too.

The coup

In the revolution era there was a coup whereby money was no longer the reigning king. Money, as the prime object, the drive, was overthrown and replaced by something else. If you doubt this, take a look at these examples:

On 18 May 2016 Richard Branson tweeted:
*"**If you're driven only by the pursuit of wealth** and fame, you've got your priorities in the wrong order, and **you don't stand much of a chance** of making it in the long term. On the other hand, **if you boldly put purpose over profit**, the latter will follow the former. I'm convinced of that."*

It's worth reading this again...: *"If you boldly put purpose over profit, the latter will follow the former" "If you're driven only by the pursuit of wealth... you don't stand much of a chance..."* Richard Branson, the global entrepreneur is telling us that purpose should reign over profit! Such a statement is inconceivable in conventional business thinking. In the link included in his tweet he added *"From the day I took my first steps as an entrepreneur, I've felt that the only mission worth pursuing in business is to **make people's lives better.**"*[6] That was the only mission that was worth pursuing in business for him. In other words, his passion and drive behind the first steps he took in business were not about making profit, but rather about making people's lives better.

This approach directly contradicts the conventional dictionary definition of an entrepreneur mentioned earlier. In the conventional definition the only mission, the only hope when setting up in business, is making profit. Whereas Richard Branson, clearly a Freedom Revolution Entrepreneur, says the exact opposite is correct. It is, he says, all about the pursuit of purpose, not profit and he is convinced of that.

This isn't the same as saying he didn't care whether his business was making a profit or not. On the contrary. Did Mr Branson want Virgin to make money? I bet you he did! Is it making money? Absolutely. But money was a desirable outcome, not the drive. It wasn't the aim. The aim was to make people's lives better and making profit followed. Of course Mr Branson set up his business way before the revolution, but I am sure it's not the first time it has been said that Richard Branson is ahead of his time.

Larry Page, co-founder of Google explains the background behind setting up Google:
*"Our intense and enduring interest was to objectively **help people find information** efficiently...From providing people with life-saving information to helping breakdown global barriers."*[7]

Money isn't mentioned anywhere. Did Mr Page want Google to make money? I am sure he did. Is Google making money? We all know the answer to that. But money was a desirable outcome, not the drive. It wasn't the aim. The aspiration was to help people find information. To save lives with that information. To breakdown global barriers. That was the drive and the profit, as we know, followed.

This was written about Bill Gates by the author J.D. Meier:
*"Bill Gates is a visionary that makes things happen by creating systems bigger than himself and inspiring people to join him on epic adventures to **change the world. He is not a seeker of fame or fortune, although he has both. He's a maker of impact.** Technology is his way, and reducing inequalities in the world is his game."*[8]

No sign of a dollar anywhere. Bill Gates is not a seeker of fame or fortune, although he has plenty of both. Did Mr Gates want Microsoft to make money? Yes he did. Is Microsoft making money? Quite a lot. But money was a desirable outcome, not the drive. It wasn't the aim. The aspiration was to take us on an epic journey to change our world. The aim was to make an impact on our lives. He succeeded in doing both and, yet again, fame and fortune followed.

Mark Zuckerberg said:
*"If you just work on stuff that you like and **you are passionate about**, you don't have to have a master plan with how things will play out"*[9]

He is not saying *'if you just work on things that will make you lots of money, you don't have to have a master plan with how things will play out'*. He is saying that if you work on matters that you are *passionate about things will play out*. I explain later on in the book how as an entrepreneur in the revolution when you work on things that you are passionate about, you arrive at your business project with a business and marketing plan already built in, which isn't the case for entreprewhores. Did Mr Zuckerberg want Facebook to make money? He certainly did. Is Facebook making money? Plenty. But money was a desirable outcome, not the drive. It wasn't the aim. The aspiration was to follow the passion and do stuff that he liked and then things just 'played out'. Have they not?

There seems to be a common theme running here. It is no longer simply about the 'one P', profit. It is about the 'three Ps' and in order of priority: passion and purpose with profit relegated to third place.

Purpose

"Purpose, Purpose- Everywhere!" exclaims Aaron Hurst with passion in his excellent book "The Purpose Economy". Entrepreneurs, he explains, **"are all driven by the pursuit of purpose** and, together, they create the Purpose Economy".[10]

It's a sentence worth repeating: entrepreneurs are all driven by the pursuit of **purpose**. Not money or profit, purpose! Again, such a statement would have been implausible before the revolution. Ask anyone walking the pre- revolution streets what entrepreneurs were driven by, and they would have undoubtedly replied, money. Indeed before the revolution we all, as people in business, were in pursuit of money.

But not anymore.

In the revolution money is no longer the drive, it is a given. Revolutionary entrepreneurs have ambitions other than money. Money was replaced by something else. But what was it replaced with?

Your freedom

In the revolution being in business is all about your freedom to pursue your dreams, passion and purpose. It is all about "your desire for impact, personal growth and community is changing the world" (The Purpose Economy).[11]

In the revolution you, the changemaker within a business or the business founder, are a creator, an artist and, by definition, you revolt. In this era, you revolt to set yourself free to pursue your purpose and dream, and then set others free to pursue theirs. You will be making money as a result but not as your prime target. This will involve financial and emotional risk as well as putting your personal reputation at stake, but your return on investment is your freedom. And that is the best ROI out there.

It is only when you are free and your business or career drive is fuelled by a purpose that is truly aligned with your passion and core values, that

25

you suddenly feel elated. You feel that working is no longer 'work', that business is pleasure and the dilemma of whether to mix them together is irrelevant as you can't tell when 'business' ends and 'pleasure' starts. They are all one. It doesn't matter what day of the week it is or, what time, you're consumed by it. You feel enlightened, present and full of consciousness. You feel alive like you have never felt before. This is when you know that freedom has trumped fear and suddenly you are the person you always knew you could be. You come up with exciting ideas that seem real and achievable and at that moment you just know you can do it!

You then throw yourself into situations that often, and for so many people, seem impossible. To the outside world it seems as though you are deliberately 'looking for trouble' and to solve these troubles you need great courage. But you wouldn't miss it for the world. You enjoy every minute of it because you are free.

Entreprewhores hope to make more profit overlooking their purpose, their calling if you wish. The Entreprewhore is missing such an enormous opportunity to change her own life and that of others. There she is stuck in the never ending rat race constantly hoping for and chasing after more profit, but with that nasty empty feeling inside of 'what's the point?'

There is a point. It was there, but it was missed. As entreprewhores we were simply bound by the many preconceptions as to what it meant to be a person in business. We were trapped and freedom was no more.

*"**Purpose is what you believe matters** as manifested in your actions- big and small."* (The Purpose Economy).[12] What was missed is what mattered, and when your actions are not aligned with what matters, there is no freedom or happiness. There is just a pursuit, a rat race and a constant need for external validation, but internally there is that hole that doesn't get filled. The writing is on the wall. What matters is no longer just higher salary, more profit or more stuff. What matters now is freedom. It is the freedom to pursue your passion and purpose that is at the forefront of this revolution.

I therefore believe that the true definition of an 'Entrepreneur', or as I call them, 'FREE Entrepreneur' is:

> "A creator and a changemaker in business who takes on reputational, emotional and financial risks to be free to pursue their passion and apply profit to make a positive impact on their life and other people's lives as a result."

I stood at the **ACUMEN** BUSINESS CONVENTION stage on 10 May 2016 in Brighton in front of nearly 300 business leaders and shared this definition with them. Eight days later Mr Branson tweeted that the *"only mission worth pursuing in business is to **make people's lives better**"* and that, *"**if you boldly put purpose over profit**, the latter will follow the former"*. He was convinced of that, he added.

It perfectly fitted the Freedom Revolution definition of a true FREE Entrepreneur that I had presented.

Changemakers within businesses

Note that my definition of FREE Entrepreneur refers to a 'creator and a changemaker in business', not simply to people who set up business/es. The latter is such a narrow minded definition because it misses out on a huge pool of influential entrepreneurial talent of changemaking in the business world.

Meg Whitman served as President and Chief Executive Officer of eBay from 1998 to 2008. During Whitman's 10 years with the company, she oversaw its expansion from 30 employees and $4 million in annual revenue, to more than 15,000 employees and $8 billion in annual revenue. In 2014, Whitman was named 20th in Forbes List of the 100 Most Powerful Women in the World.

Is she not an entrepreneur?

Alex Ferguson won 38 trophies, 13 Premier League titles, 5 FA Cups and 2 Champion League titles. Yes football might be a game, but it is first and foremost a business, a colossal one too.

Isn't Ferguson, the longest serving manager of Manchester United, an entrepreneur?

Whilst these are global examples, and there are so many more, if you look around, you will also see changemakers in your own business community, maybe even in your own business. Truly FREE Entrepreneurs who are taking on reputational, emotional and financial risks to be free to pursue their passion and apply the fruit of their success to make a positive impact on their life and other people's lives as a result. I am immensely proud to work with such changemakers within Acumen who have done extraordinary things throughout the years. They, too, are true FREE Entrepreneurs.

As a FREE Entrepreneur, whether as a founder or a changemaker within a business, you will face difficulties, there will be downs as well as ups and sometimes it will end in tears, but you will be free. Free to put your purpose over profit, to make your life and other people's lives better and make money along the way to ensure you can do it again and again.

What is it that really matters to you that you may be missing? Do you know what it is? Do you know what your passion is? Your purpose? Do you know where you can find it?

In your dreams!
We all have our daydream life in mind and in that dream, we enjoy what we do and everything we do fits in with our lives in great harmony. To quote Mahatma Gandhi: *"Happiness is when what you think, what you say and what you do are in harmony."* Our daydream thoughts, therefore, ought to be spoken and carried through in harmony for us to be truly happy. But to think, speak and act in harmony, you must first be free to even dare to dream of it, let alone speak of it and execute it.

Consider your daydreams and you will see they are made of a sense of purpose that is only meaningful to you. That sense of purpose is always, without exception, aligned with your core values and when that combination takes place, what you see in abundance is what people refer to as 'passion', 'drive' and 'enthusiasm'. These daydreams are in your thoughts. You speak of them in a special way. You experience extraordinary feelings when you follow them; the feelings of happiness, of bliss, of freedom. Feelings that are seldom experienced.

Are you ready to literally follow your dream, to be free? What is it that is stopping you? Do you believe dreams are for dreamers not realists? Or maybe you are not sure what your passion is? You aren't certain what your purpose is? Then twist the question on its head, what is your biggest frustration? Often frustration is the flip side of passion. Flip it. What can you see?

Give this some considered thought. Your responses will affect every decision you make in your business and life. They have certainly affected mine.

Chapter 3
Your Dream Frustration

D reams are often borne of frustration which can prove to be a positive thing. It is the frustration that sometimes fills you with an overflowing sense of purpose. It inspires you to embark on a mission to correct them, make them better, and change them. And this is your first step to becoming a changemaker.

In the following pages I share my personal changemaking journey with you, the aim being to trigger thoughts within you about your own journey. Whilst my story relates to my experience in the legal sector, it involves the same or very similar principles that apply to most businesses. These anecdotes should be used to help you reflect on your journey, your industry and your business project. Doing that should hopefully inspire you to get on your changemaking path to ensure that, in your case too, profit follows passion.

Because that's how we've always done it

So many successful business stories start with a passion to resolve a frustration. Such frustrations became prominent to me as I was climbing up my invisible career ladder. For years I felt the legal industry was lagging behind the rest of the business world. Even though I worked for excellent modern firms before setting up **ACUMEN** BUSINESS LAW, I felt that on certain levels more than just a few lawyers were acting as aloof HMRC clerks rather than as commercially minded people in business. There is too often a distant culture of lawyers with regard to their clients that doesn't seem to exist in any other industry. More often than not you would see lawyers who either genuinely believe, or are very good at giving the impression that they are smarter and better and that frankly clients sometimes just get in their way. So they avoid them by hiding behind a battery of secretaries or trainees.

This culture manifests itself in many aspects of behaviour. For example, instead of picking up the phone or sending an email, the lawyer regularly dictates a four line letter. The dictated transcript gets handed over to a secretary to be typed, who then hands it back to the lawyer to make final amendments and then, once the letter is finalised, it gets printed (on real paper), signed (with real ink), folded (manually by real hands), put in an envelope, stamped and finally posted. This is not a strange anecdote, an odd behaviour here and there or some crazy one-off experience. This was the done thing, and it still is in so many law firms. This was the done thing for me too before I joined the revolution and set myself free. But even though that was my experience nearly a decade ago, it still astonishes me how often this still happens. To this day we receive letters comprising one or two paragraphs from the other side's solicitors on a regular basis.

Why? It is a new millennium! Pick up the phone, send a text, an email or better still get on with the work. I find it so patronising to clients and it makes absolutely no sense. It is the opposite of a win-win. It is a 'lose-lose' situation for the client, the client's business, the lawyer and the law firm. Cynics say the reason is that it justifies a bill as all the above kafuffle generates more minutes of work that can be turned into money. But what damage to the client relationship does it cause when the client can see that the lawyer couldn't be bothered to pick up the phone or send an email, preferring instead to send a superfluous letter?

At **ACUMEN** BUSINESS LAW we made a decision from the outset not to have secretaries. We have an outstanding Operations Manager and two one-year placement law students who provide us with all round support, including administrative. Each one of us personally calls, writes and talks directly to our clients; no dicta phone in sight and it all works beautifully.

The point to reflect on here is that just because that's how you've always done something, doesn't mean you should unquestioningly continue with no change, with no re-evaluation. Maybe that habit is no longer in line with modern times, with your brand or your purpose. Put your business habits under the microscope. What is it that you do in a certain way simply because that's how you've always done it? Is there a better alternative? Better for your clients, colleagues, business, you?

I know too well that it is not always easy to break away from long standing traditions and business habits. But doing so means you can identify all those habits that no longer work, cause frustration and need fixing. It is this process that turns frustrations into passion and gives us a purpose.

We lawyers have deep rooted commercial habits going back hundreds of years that I had to challenge, one such habit being the way we charge.

How much would you pay me to talk to you about the weather?
Not much I am guessing. But it is very likely that every time you speak to your lawyer you are doing exactly that. Indeed the ingrained charging method of legal fees was one of my main frustrations with the legal industry. Lawyers charge by an hourly rate which to me seems to go against any business common sense, especially for non-contentious matters (i.e. when no one is fighting anyone but where one simply needs a business document such as a shareholders' agreement, terms & conditions, a lease, employment contract, trademark, staff handbook, etc.). When charging by the hour, lawyers take sixty minutes and divide it by ten units of six minutes each. You are then charged for every minute the lawyer spends working on your matter. And I mean, every minute. Be it drafting emails, meetings attendance, or talking to you on the phone. Not surprisingly, the instructions in every client's office are 'don't call the lawyer unless you really have to' because they pay for every minute the lawyer spends talking to them. And I, for example, can talk quite a lot.

How can a lawyer foster a relationship with her clients if they would much rather not talk to her at all if possible? How can she truly engage with the client's business? How can she make sure she understands the bigger picture if there is justifiable pressure from the client to keep the time spent to a minimum?

Therefore when I was in the process of setting up **ACUMEN** BUSINESS LAW, I took the decision to scrap the hourly rate charging system and to quote fixed fees at the outset for all non-contentious matters instead. My friends, a few of whom are lawyers, strongly advised me against this. The main reason being that this is how it is done by all law firms so it must be for a good reason.

Is there a 'done thing' in your industry that is still being done by all because 'it must be for a good reason'?

The lawyers warned me that clients would abuse it as they would be constantly on the phone to me, intimating this is a bad thing. I talk about 'family and friends' advice' later on but whilst there is no doubt they meant well, they didn't share my purpose. They didn't share my passion of changing the way business law services are provided in the market place, preferring instead the status quo. They couldn't understand that abolishing the hourly rate charging system for all non-contentious matters was perfectly aligned with my purpose and, as such, was the right thing for me to do.

Your family and friends no doubt mean well too, but they are unlikely to share your passion, have the same core values and be driven by the same purpose.

I remember when the business was in its early weeks of trading looking through the Law Society Gazette which had arrived that morning. Inside was a double page article about a magic circle City law firm. They had instructed some top international consultants to advise them on changes they should make to help improve their law firm. The conclusion was there in the headline in big bold letters; 'CLIENTS PREFER FIXED FEES'. It was a triumphant moment for me. I had no authority, not one client to my name and yet I felt quite smug thinking to myself *'they should have asked me, I would have told them that for a lot less!'*

And so I strongly recommend you make a list of what frustrates you in your industry:

- What in your industry do clients not like?
- What is not working that well?
- What is not aligned with the rest of the changes that are happening in the world?

It doesn't have to be a particularly long list. In fact I recommend you start with the top five substantial issues you find frustrating in your industry.

I also made such a list before I set up my firm and amongst my top frustrations were the charging method and the aloof culture I mentioned previously. But also up there at the top was the lack of passion that some business lawyers have to, well, business…

If the client's business is none of yours, you are missing the point
I remember going to a meeting with my boss as a junior lawyer. The client was looking to have employment contracts drafted. My boss was effectively a clerk filling in a form. How many employees? What's the holiday entitlement? Pension? Company car? When the client left I asked my boss *'what do they actually do?'* His reply was *'I don't know, selling some widgets'*. There was absolutely no interest in the client as a business person or her company as a business. There was a completely blinkered approach of *'I am here to execute a task of drafting employment contracts and that it is all I am going to concern myself with'*. And my boss was a good lawyer and a very nice person. He was not unusual. He was the norm.

The documents are meaningless without regard to the people they are supposed to make a difference to. Legal documents in isolation are extremely dull (I am sure I have not shattered any preconceptions in saying that). However, the very same legal documents or, in your case, your products or services, come to life when you know their true purpose; when you know the people behind them, why they are looking to rely on them and, most importantly, when you understand and truly care about their dreams.

But most service providers, lawyers in particular, are not trained to be interested in their clients' business dreams. You are not taught these matters when you get your qualification or, if you are a lawyer, when you read your law degree. Service providers are there, in their eyes, to give professional advice and bill for it. That's a shame because so many are missing the third and very important reason that links providing any professional advice with billing for it, legal or otherwise.

Some service providers miss the opportunity to become a partner in their client's business. Not a partner in the legal sense where they own part of the business, but a person who takes part in their journey that they can trust. When a client truly feels her advisors have joined her journey by virtue of their conduct, the advisor has that relationship for life. But the advisor can't simply pay lip service to this on their website and in their marketing literature. They must show it in every single one of their actions. Partnerships that are built on this basis make the working life so much more enjoyable and they result in you providing a much better service to your clients and their business in the process. This will earn more than the unnecessary four-line dictated letter ever will, if you are a lawyer, or any other superfluous act or product if you're not.

Caring about a client's business, which is very often their baby and a reflection of their dream, was so important to me when I set up my firm. To ensure we were on board as a partner of our clients from the very outset we introduced a new process and named it the 'Legal MoT'® which is also our registered trademark. When clients come to see us for, say, an employment contract, we will certainly discuss the employment contract with them, but we start by taking a step back and asking the client to tell us about their business. Changemakers love talking about their business, particularly to people who are genuinely interested in listening.

How can you get your changemaker clients to talk to you about their business when you interact with them? What helpful questions can you raise and what tips could you share without charging?

To make sure there is no doubt we are genuinely interested, we do not charge for the Legal MoT® meeting. This way we actively *show*, as opposed to just *say*, that we are genuinely interested in the client's business. We demonstrate in our actions that the Legal MoT® is not a marketing trick to get the client talking so the meeting is longer and we can charge more, as may be done by the entrepre*whore* who is in pursuit of profit and nothing else. When you are seeking freedom to pursue your purpose and passion, there is no hidden agenda; you do what is aligned with your core values and the profit follows.

Once you have meaningful conversations with clients where you are genuinely listening, you learn so much about their business as well as about the person sitting opposite you. This of course helps you to advise them better too. During the Legal MoT® it sometimes becomes apparent that in fact it is not an employment contract for example that they need, but actually a freelancer agreement or, maybe, there are other fundamental matters that need addressing more urgently than the employment contract. Conclusions we could not have arrived at without caring about the client and their business in the first place. Because it is only when you genuinely care that you ask the right questions.

You will see in the appendix that I have added a section with your own Legal MoT®. I am a business lawyer after all so I couldn't quite let you go without some legal gems to protect your business. But in a nutshell, the Legal MoT® provides our clients with a dashboard snapshot of where their business stands from a legal point of view. It tells them how legally protected their business is. We have had clients that have worked with other law firms for several years leaving our office after the initial Legal MoT® meeting saying '*I have learned more today about the legal side of my business than in 10 years with my previous lawyers*'. For us that translates to '*you really do care about me and my business*'. Bingo! There is the sense of freedom, right there. Passion and purpose meeting the desired outcome. Bliss. Did income follow? Of course. But that was never the intended purpose when we developed the Legal MoT®. Nevertheless it is very often the outcome.

What processes can you introduce that will make your clients feel you really care about their business and that will be genuinely helpful to them?

That will make you stand out from your competitors as it will show that you have a deeper level of understanding of their business challenges?

We are not paying you to think outside your box
Up there on my list of frustrations was the disregard many businesses have to the most valuable gift that will ever exist in their business.

They have this valuable gift staring them in the face, every minute of the working day. And yet it is constantly overlooked. Most industries are guilty of this. This gift does not usually require further financial investment. It just needs you to firstly notice it as a gift and to then genuinely care about it. The gift I am referring to is your colleagues' essence, not their professional ability. You are probably well aware of this. I am referring to *their* dreams, purpose and aspiration. Yes they have those too.

The terms boss, shareholders, directors, employees, freelancers, etc. are all extremely important from a *legal* point of view, but they are fundamental distractions from a commercial and human interaction point of view and they are limiting. Open the window and throw them all out! Why? Because they cloud your judgment. They blinker your vision and crucially you miss out on the most wonderful experiences simply because you are paying too much attention to these titles.

So many businesses simply look at the people in their business as 'capability cadets'. '*Doug does the coding, Jane does the design, James does Copyright Law and Vanessa is Head of Accounts*'. But before Doug, Jane, James and Vanessa specialised and were given these titles they were, and they still are, people. It sounds obvious doesn't it, yet most businesses overlook this. Doug, Jane, James and Vanessa are a bundle of energy, with life experiences, thoughts, dreams and ideas. Everyone has ideas. There is no such thing as a person without ideas. There are only people with fear, something we talk about later.

In my previous jobs we would have team meetings where secretaries would be conspicuous by their absence. I remember at a meeting in one of the law firms I was working for at the time, the team agreed to run a seminar. We wanted the secretary to look into catering. One of the partners came out of the meeting and asked the secretary to '*look into catering for 20 people in November please*'. How much in your opinion do you think she cared about that catering? Very little. Would you care much if the task was presented to you as such? It is nothing but a chore, but nevertheless it is part of her job so she has to 'get on with it'. Sadly it is that lack of engagement you are going to get if you fail to inspire the person by involving them in the decision making process and the discussions at the very outset.

So how different would it be if the secretary had been in the meeting, not as a guest or as a one off gesture, but as an equal member of the team just like the lawyers present? In fact, what if it was the secretary who suggested a seminar with catering to help attract attendees? If it was her idea and everyone agreed it was a brilliant one, would she be more likely to care about the task of sourcing the catering? Absolutely. Better still, if, say, she knew the precise details of the department's budget and how tricky it would be to stretch it to fund the seminar and the catering, would she be more likely to do her utmost to see her idea come to life by finding a catering firm that could match the budget? I am certain she would. The difference in the manner in which she would have engaged is so vast with so many positive future ripple effects, it is beyond measurement.

But guess what? Not only have you missed an opportunity to make your event much more special because the secretary really couldn't care less, but you just killed her dream. It may be that hospitality is one of her passions. When people come to her family home, she loves making it look and feel really special. She loves it that she is known amongst her friends and family as 'the hostess with the mostest'. What would that do to you if you were being ignored in this way about something you are passionate about? What if this happened on a regular basis week after week, month after month? How many parts inside you would die in the process? Bit by bit your dreams are shattered.

Seeing this done to people, including me where I wasn't involved because my title didn't seem relevant or I was not deemed important enough, were by far the most frustrating experiences that I was hoping in my dreams to fix. But dreams are for dreamers right? So I wiped them out with *stop trying to fix the world*' sentiments and got on with my job.

You can see how the list of examples of my frustrations related to systems and processes that existed in my industry for years. That was the way lawyers and law firms had always conducted themselves but I nevertheless permitted myself to question them. I questioned all I could and although not everything needed changing and not everything was frustrating, I acted upon those that did. I turned the frustrations into innovation in my business.

I invite you to do the same in your business:

- What is it about your industry that clients don't like?
- What is common practice, but really doesn't have to be?
- What is happening in your business, your team, your project that may be killing people's passions and aspirations?
- What level of engagement will you get from people if they were truly involved and if their opinions really mattered?
- What would it do to your business, your team or your project if you respected people's passion and engagement and helped make their work dreams come true?
- Most importantly, *how would you change people's lives?*

Changing people's lives for the better- your clients', your colleagues' and yours- is what the Freedom Revolution is all about. If you approach it from the angle of *'how can I manipulate my clients and colleagues' dreams to increase my profits?'* you have missed the entire point and in the long run it won't work. That is not the mindset of a changemaker, it is that of an entreprewhore.

You need to genuinely aspire to change people's lives for the better, to set them free for **their** benefit! As Nelson Mandela famously said: *"For to be free, is not merely to cast off one's chains, but to live in a way that respects and enhances the freedom of others"*.[13]

So there was the list of my frustrations, the flip side of which formed the foundation of my dreams. I passionately wanted to be part of a law firm that was *genuinely* different, with a unique DNA. A firm that would partner with its clients, care about their businesses and about them as business people. I wanted my firm to value the mammoth input each person in the organisation was capable of providing. I wanted to ditch and ignore the archaic titles of boss, shareholders, directors, employees, and freelancer, etc. preferring instead to recognise that everyone, no exceptions, has a dream and that together we could create something quite powerful. Together, we could be changemakers.

My day dream was aligned with my core values. It reflected what I believed mattered from the bottom of my heart and I wanted badly to manifest in my actions. I wanted my thoughts, my words and my action to coincide in harmony, as this is what happiness is all about. I wanted to be free to live this life I was daydreaming about.

So it was time to get on that horse, carry that flag and lead a change, right?

Well not quite.

Chapter 4
Negative Sinking

There are two types of people to be aware of: the 'why yes' people - those who instinctively think of all the positive reasons to do something, and the 'why not' people - those who instinctively think of all the negative reasons why not to do something. The latter outnumber the former substantially. It is not about 'good people' and 'bad people' or even right or wrong, it is just the way people are and there are reasons for it, some are discussed below.

But even the 'why yes' people will frequently raise 'why not' questions before deciding to go ahead and do something. Top this with the fact that the answers to the 'why not' questions always seem more reasonable and convincing, it comes as no surprise that so few of us are free to pursue our dream.

When I was experiencing the many frustrations in the legal industry and dreaming about correcting them, I was in the 'why yes' mode.

'Why yes'?

Because I was passionate about changing the way in which business legal services are provided and purchased in the market place for the better. Because I wanted to create a better working environment for people where they could work together, inspire, be inspired, be truly empowered to make a difference; where they too could follow their own dreams. Because I wanted to help clients realise their dreams. Because I was interested in business, the people behind them and their passion. Because there had got to be another better way!

'Why not'?

Because I was a partner in an established firm with a good salary. Because trying to innovate in the legal industry was a lost cause. Because the legal industry doesn't like change and I would be mocked and undermined. Because I had a shoestring budget. Because I had no potential partners to set up the firm with and going it alone was unwise. Because ethically and morally I didn't want to poach clients from my previous firm so I would have to start from scratch. Because there were so many established law firms around me, their phones ringing merely by virtue of their existence. Because I only specialised in commercial contracts so I wouldn't be able to offer the full range of business law services. Because it would be so hard. Because we were experiencing the worst recession in decades. Because I had a new born baby and two other young children. Because I was the main breadwinner.

Because I had just been diagnosed with a rare and aggressive form of cancer and had been told I might not survive.

What sounds more convincing? The 'why yes' or the 'why not' arguments? Some pie in the sky dream about fixing the world, or a list with proper practical logical reasons? Of course the latter, it always does, because the former is your dream and the latter is your reality. So you tuck the dream away and carry on doing what you have always done, but nevertheless still hoping for a change. That's what I did on so many occasions over the years. It was only when I was pregnant with my third child, clearly the worst possible time as far as the 'why not' department is concerned, that I snapped out of the 'why not' for good. I was going to follow my passion and purpose. I was going to be free.

It is all in your head

The belief I am about to share I know to be true. I have seen it proven time and time again in my life and the lives of those around me. Not only does it manifest itself in relation to business, but also in all aspects of our lives such as relationships and money, even the future.

Almost everything you say, do and believe about yourself is the result of your perception. What you think of your essence, namely your spirit, core, heart, quintessence, is only how you perceive it to be. There is no 'absolute truth' about who you are, the kind of life you should live, relationships you may have, the career or business you may run, how much money you should have, even how your future will be shaped. If you are passionate about pursuing another role in your career and your boss/mum/friend says you are not suited to it, this may be true only in that this is their view. It is not the *absolute truth* as to whether you are suited to the role or not. If one client says he will pay you £500 for your service, then this is true in relation to how much money that client will pay you, but it is not the *absolute truth* as to how much money you can earn or what your service is worth. Similarly when you say '*I don't have enough money*' or '*my business is a small business*' or '*my relationship isn't working*', these are not absolute truths. They are merely your perception of the current state of affairs.

Often a large part of your perception comprises the 'I am too [fill in the blank]' sentence. We are all champions at telling ourselves why we are too 'something'. I am too short, tall, ugly, pretty, fat, thin, funny, casual, boring, dull, weird, perfectionist to.... do whatever it is you've just convinced yourself you can't.

The famous quote of Henry Ford summarises this theory perfectly: "*If you think you can or you think you can't, you are right*". It is all in your mind. It is all your perception.

I hear you say '*Well that is not quite true. It is not just about my perception, there are other external contributing factors that shape my life such as economic climate, upbringing, money, contacts, having children*'. The list goes on. To that I will say, yes you are absolutely correct, these are all important contributing factors, but that is all they are. They are 'contributing factors' they are not 'absolute truths' because if they were, then no one would be thriving in a bad economic climate, or if they had a tough upbringing; if they are a parent or poor.

But when you look around you see so many people thriving precisely under such conditions. So many people from all walks of life throughout history, be they famous business tycoons, successful people in the media, academics or leading politicians have been immensely successful despite such limiting factors applying to their lives. Is that not the case? Surely that's impossible?

But it is not. Because *"Impossible is just a big word thrown around by small men who find it easier to live in the world they've been given than to explore the power they have to change it. Impossible is not a fact. It's an opinion. Impossible is not a declaration. It's a dare. Impossible is potential. Impossible is temporary. Impossible is nothing"* (Muhammad Ali).

What do they have that others don't?
Fundamentally, what they have and others don't is a better dictionary. There is one major difference between happy, contented and successful people and those who are not. All the former, without exception, use a liberating dictionary and the latter use a limiting one. Consider these four examples:

	Limiting dictionary	Liberating dictionary
LIFE	Life is tough	Life hands lemons, I make lemonade
MONEY	Money doesn't grow on trees	The streets are paved with gold
BUSINESS	It is a very competitive market	There is plenty to go around
FUTURE	Bring back the good old days	Tomorrow is another day!

Who do you think is likely to build a more successful business? The person who thinks it is a very competitive market or the one who believes there is plenty to go around? What actions and decisions are you likely to take if you are the business person who thinks that:

- Money doesn't grow on trees
- Money is the root of all evil
- I have to work hard for the money
- I am not talented enough to earn that much/ grow my business
- I don't like how rich people are and if I become rich I will become one of them...

If these are your thoughts and observations, what kind of mindset will you have? What habits will you develop as a consequence? What decisions will you make in your business and career?

I set up **ACUMEN** BUSINESS LAW in September 2007. Several weeks later the whole world collapsed around me, or so it felt. 'The worst economic downturn since the 1920s' screamed the newspaper headlines. Two established law firms closed their Brighton branches at around the same time I set up my firm. Had I used a limiting dictionary I wouldn't have stood a chance. I was the main breadwinner, with three young children; I had just finished my six months' maternity leave and had been treated for my cancer by the Marsden Hospital in London. I was on a shoestring budget; not one client to my name and right in the middle of the worst recession of my lifetime.

All I had to work with was a liberating dictionary, my purpose and passion; nothing more.

Using the liberating dictionary doesn't imply you bury your head in the sand. I acknowledged there was a recession and simply made a conscious decision not to participate in it. I decided there was still *plenty* to go round I simply had to ensure that some of it came my way.

Thoughts >>> Mindset >>> Habits >>> Decision Making >>> Reality
So many people wrongly see their definition of their essence, of who they are, as an absolute truth. They impose their own made up rules, limits and laws about what they can do, have or be. The worst thing of all is that these negative self imposed definitions, made up rules and limits end up dictating how your essence will manifest in practice. They become a self fulfilling prophecy. 'Surely, I can only earn this much for my skills'. But there is no law which says that (I have checked!).

These are your laws and if they are limiting then they can and should be broken.

It all starts with one thought. Always. Did you know that we think 48 thoughts per minute? That is approximately 70,000 thoughts per day(!) That is 490,000 thoughts in one week and in a year that amounts to over 25 million thoughts! All these thoughts combined create a story in our mind. This is how we report back to ourselves. It can be immensely powerful but equally it can be terribly destructive. If most of your 70,000 thoughts are based on the limiting dictionary, how do you think your life will look? What would be your absolute truth? If you have an idea for your career or for setting up in business, and all these thoughts are coming into your head straight from the limiting dictionary, what is the likelihood of your idea materialising let alone being successful?

These thoughts reside permanently inside us. They create habits which then lead to decisions we make that become our reality.

If you are satisfied with how the essence is manifested in your life, then you have created the absolute truth that works for you and makes you happy. Therefore, nothing should be changed. But if you are not satisfied, the good news is that it is all in your mind and, as such, in your complete control. You don't need anything external such as money or permission from another person to change it. However you do have a challenge ahead of you because unsurprisingly changing habits is one of our toughest challenges.

Ask yourself, and please don't be shy. No one is listening and you will not be judged:

- What is your dream? Your passion? Your purpose?
- How do you want your career or business to look/be/operate?
- What is the financial reality you want to live in, however grand?
- How do you want your life to look?
- What kind of relationships do you want to have with the people around you?
- What do you want your future to look like?

Remember there are no rules as to what the answers can or can't be. They can only be what you want. Then ask yourself this very important question:

What are in your thoughts, mindset and habits that are conflicting with the reality you desire?

If you identify something in your thoughts/ mindset/ habits that is conflicting with the reality you are trying to achieve then make a deal with yourself today to take one step towards changing it. What one step can you take towards changing a state of affairs that you are unhappy with? If you could make just one change, what would it be? What thought pattern will you need to adopt to bring about that change?

And remember - it all starts with one thought! Just let that one good thought in and you will be on your way. Will you dare?

Fear

I have to dare you because you are scared. We are all scared. Fear is one of the most influential factors in our decision making process, particularly the fear of the unknown.

Fear can be paralysing.

It doesn't matter how many times we tell ourselves before making a decision *'don't worry it might never happen'*, all we can think is - *'yes, but what if it does happen?!'*

I had many reasons to be fearful before making the decision to leave my career as a partner and set up in business. Every reason was valid, factual and logical. But I was equally passionate about my dream and armed with my liberating dictionary and positive mindset, I refused to go down the road of negative sinking in the fear mud. So how do we make that fear go away? How can we overcome it?

The way I deal with fear is to firstly bring everything to a halt, just for a few minutes. I stop and silence the fear storm in my head and stare at the fear right in the eyes. I then think about the risks involved that give rise to the fear. When you do this what you will find is that very often the risks you fear, when you stop and really think about them aren't actually that risky. Just stop and ask yourself: 'what is the worst that can happen?' Very often the answer includes things like: a little inconvenience, embarrassment, an unpleasant feeling of failure and maybe the loss of some money. But nothing which is life destroying. Often you realise that even if it didn't work, nonetheless this time next year you will be way over most if not all of it. You realise that 'the worst that can happen' isn't bad enough to warrant giving up on your dreams.

Then what you often find is that the main reason fear exists is because maybe, on that occasion, in relation to that project, you believe that you can't achieve the thing for which you need to take the risk. Then we are back to the mindset point. If you can rid yourself of your perceptions, of the things you value as absolute truths and hold on tight to the liberating dictionary, you will start believing that you can do it and that the answer to the 'what's the worst that can happen' question, is that it isn't actually that bad. What happens then? The fear fades away. It is still there, but now in the background.

And then ask yourself an even better question - what's the best that can happen? And now, when you are imagining the best happening, isn't it just great?

It is also worth remembering that fear often revolves around money. But the beauty of the Freedom Revolution, as we saw and as we will see in more detail later on, is that money follows passion. Remember? Profit follows purpose and passion. Being in the revolution therefore means that you're far better equipped to deal with fear.

Fear - friends and family

Once we manage to overcome fear, we usually feel highly motivated and what do we do next? We go and tell, and sometimes also consult with, our friends and family. What do you think happens then? What do you think their mindset is likely to be? They are as insecure as you, as the rest of us. They have their own fears. They love and care about you, so their fear intensifies because they strongly feel they have to protect you. Combine all this with the fact they are most likely not that passionate about your purpose, then unsurprisingly their advice or reaction is 'I'm not sure this is going to work'. Armed with their own limiting dictionary and with their lack of passion to your cause, they end up projecting their own fears back at you.

So if you want to prepare a gourmet meal and your friend is a cook, by all means do consult him for some tips. If you need a bank loan and your sister is a banker, give her a call. But if you have a dream to pursue your purpose and passion remember - the bucks stop with you.

What a powerful and liberating thought!

Sod the odds
Despite the odds being stacked against me, I decided to give it a go. I went from a partner's salary to earning no money at all. I replaced the prestigious, hard earned title of 'Partner' with 'self-employed', 'one woman band' or, the not so glamorous 'sole practitioner'. From working for top 100 law firms, I was now working for a firm that no one even bothered to count and from head of department, I now had no team or colleagues. It was just me on my own.

I remember just after moving into my new office inviting a friend to visit. I showed her around feeling very proud and excited: 'look this is going to be the boardroom and this is where I will be sitting. Look I bought a computer, a phone, post it notes in yellow and in pink!' 'Oh wow that's great', she replied, 'and what about clients?' 'Oh yes, that...'. Well I had none.

But for the first time in my career I had a purpose of a type I had never experienced before. I had a real passion and desire to follow my dream of *changing the way in which business law services were provided and purchased in the market place*. The title, status and pay, they had fallen off my radar. I was excited! I was going to give it my all! I was going to give it whatever it took. You can do this because when you are free nothing that relates to your passion is ever a chore. Your passion is your calling. You live it. You can't stop thinking about it. You want to make it better, superior, easier to use or interact with. You want to tell everyone about it. You want it loved.

Nothing or no one will get in your way. I was determined to get on with it and make it a success.

Chapter 5
Happiness

What is success?
In most business books the word 'success' or 'successful' tends to feature a lot. When I give business talks, I always make a point of discussing 'success' right at the outset. What does it actually mean, I ask?

The Google dictionary definition of 'success' is "*the accomplishment of an aim or a purpose.*" So why, especially in the business world, does success have a different meaning altogether? Why is it that Richard Branson is clearly successful to all but your window cleaner, your local architect or accountant isn't?

If your '*aim or purpose*' was to, say, leave your job and work three days a week from home as a freelancer earning around the same income as you are earning now and you achieved it, then you are, in my view, incredibly successful. You had an aim, you took steps to achieve it and you did. You are truly successful. But if your 'aim or purpose' was, say, to leave your job and set up an international global cooperation and you end up working from home three days a week as a freelancer earning about the same income as when you were an employee, then you are not successful (yet). Even though both are identical outcomes, you are successful in one but unsuccessful in the other because with the latter, you have not yet 'accomplished your aim' and, therefore, according to your own definition of success, you are not yet successful.

In other words, success is the accomplishment of an aim that you set. Not an aim set by others, be it friends, family or complete strangers.

My aim was, and still is, to change the way in which business law services are provided and purchased in the market place. To achieve this I had to offer all areas of business law services which meant I couldn't remain a sole practitioner. I also knew that to make a significant change to the way in which business law services are purchased and provided in the market place, I had to grow because as a sole practitioner the change would not be significant enough. I knew I had to grow a business in order to be successful under my definition, but does this intrinsically mean I will also be happy?

Are your settings on happy?
All human beings want to be happy. We may each have a different definition of 'happiness', but fundamentally we all want to be happy. However, even though being happy is the most predominant and universal feeling sought by the entire human race, it is often seen as a bonus, at best, or completely overlooked at worst.

Happiness is the essence of the Freedom Revolution.

In this revolution the days are gone in which making money came first but being happy in the process was somewhere down the list, if at all. This revolution is all about happiness. The freedom to pursue your purpose, your passion, your dream, is all about being happy.

Many parents will tell you that having their child was the happiest day of their life. If you are a parent you know the sense of joy that children give.

But you also know it can be difficult too. All those sleepless nights that seem to go on forever; the tears (and that's just you, not to mention the children), stress and so much worry for their well being, but somehow it is one of the most joyful experiences. It is always your bundle of joy and you wouldn't have it any other way. Some of your happiest moments are when you see that your child is happy.

The project or business you are responsible for as a changemaker in a business or as the founder is your baby and you will be going through very similar experiences. Here too, there will be sleepless nights, tears, stress and worry, but somehow you still feel that great sense of joy. Here too, some of your happiest moments are when you see happiness in your business; when you see that your colleagues, clients, suppliers and contacts are happy within your business, that 'the business is happy' in the sense that it is doing well, you will experience immense joy and satisfaction.

It is this sense of happiness that I am referring to. If you don't have it in your business life, something isn't right. You have to ensure happiness is back at the top of your list, where it should be. The good news is that if you have joined the revolution, then you are following your purpose and your dream and, therefore, by definition your settings are on 'happy'. It will sometimes go up and sometimes down, but like a thermostat it will always reset itself back onto the 'happy settings'.

So nothing can possibly go wrong. Or can it?

The journey
Things go wrong when people believe that only when they are successful, can they truly be happy. I recall having a lunch meeting with an accountant. It was by far one of the most depressing meetings I have had to date. Not because he was an accountant (now then!) but because of his approach to happiness. On the face of it, there was nothing unusual about his life. He was married and spoke fondly of his wife, had two grown up children, one in university the other one travelling. He owned a house (which I had no reason to believe he wasn't happy with) and had a good job at an accountancy firm. But one of the first things he would tell you when you spoke to him was the exact period of time he had left to his retirement, to the day! But he had over five years to go! The only time

his eyes sparkled was when he spoke about his retirement plans. He was convincing himself that the five years, eight months and six days he had left to retirement were within his reach; he was nearly there.

He needed a hug.

If you are on holiday and you send a work email or a photo of your hotel pool to your colleagues at work, there will be some people who will say 'how sad, he is on holiday and he contacts work'. Obviously the kind of people who think it is 'sad' have unfulfilling jobs at best, or jobs they hate so much that experiencing negative feelings about them is the norm. It is not surprising therefore that for such people any contact with work brings about a negative feeling and will certainly be a holiday spoiler. Now you tell me, who is actually 'sad'? The person who enjoys his working life so much so that for him to send an email to his workmates is quite fun, or the person who is sad 365 days a year minus weekends and annual holiday? Who is sadder; the person whose job happily and naturally entwines with his life or the accountant who dislikes every minute of his working day and whose life will only properly begin when he retires in five years, eight months and six days?

If you don't enjoy the journey, it isn't worth it! If you take just a handful of things from my book, let this line be one of them. I am not suggesting you should be happy every single minute of every day and that every day is a carnival along the journey. As we said there will be tough times, but on the whole you should love what you do and be happy whilst doing it. The biggest trap is to set an aim with the view that 'until I get there I am not going to bother with fluffy stuff like happiness. It may be tough and horrible but boy it will be great when I get there.' If you do this you are just like the accountant and that's not a good place to be in. If you have joined the revolution, then you will be happy because this is what the revolution is all about. So my concern is not your lack of happiness in general, but rather for you not to lose sight of happiness as you journey to your purpose.

As you know this is also true of life in general. If we keep waiting for the next stage and the next stage and the next stage to be happy, we may only start enjoying life in our 70s. What a waste! Moreover, I bet we wouldn't enjoy it even then because, by that point, 'enjoyment' means waiting for the next thing, and the next thing is, well, death. There is nothing to wait for anymore.

The exact same principle applies to your business. Do not compromise or agree to postpone your happiness for a significant length of time. Make enjoyment of the journey an integral and important part of your aim.

Happiness comes in many shapes
I was 21 years old on holiday in Tiberius in Israel. I stayed with my then boyfriend, now my husband, in cheap but lovely accommodation by the Sea of Galilee. We decided one day to head to town for the morning. We had a nice time in town, but we had not kept our finances under proper control. We had very little money and when we counted what we had left, we realised we had not left enough money for the bus fare back to the accommodation. We had a bit more money in the room, but that was of no use to us there.

The time was 2.00pm, the hottest time of the day, and the thought of a two hour walk in 33 degrees (in the shade!) back to the accommodation was really not appealing. We were annoyed with ourselves, sweating, hungry, thirsty and not very happy. As we started the dreaded walk back, we spotted a little lottery booth in the street and saw that the fee for one scratch card was exactly the sum we had. We both agreed we were going to try our luck. We had nothing to lose! The old man (well he looked old to me then; he is probably my age now...), looked bored, hot and bothered in his little air conditioned booth as he handed the scratch card to us. With shaking hands we scratched the various boxes on the card only to discover we had won enough to cover two bus tickets: and even the cost of the card too!

We screamed with joy! We jumped up and down, waved our arms about and hugged each other. We were so happy. The man looked at us a little shocked but mainly confused and said 'you do realise you only won that amount?' Of course we did! But that was all we wanted and we succeeded. After all, as we said, this is what happiness is all about.

The ride back on the bus felt like no other. Even flying business class many (many) years later didn't feel half as joyful, although admittedly twice as comfortable, as that bus ride back to our little room by the Sea of Galilee. It was then I knew that happiness comes in many shapes and forms. It all depends on your dream.

So what are you dreaming about? What will make you jump with joy and wave your arms about? What must your scratch card reveal?

Part II

In a World of Black & White, Be Ginger

"Why fit in when you were born to stand out?"

Dr Seuss

Ten Question Quiz to Determine:
How Ginger Are You?

Before you continue reading, let's have a little quiz.

No one will know your answers it is just you here, so be true. Complete the quiz now before reading the rest of the book and promise not to peep at the Ginger Scoring Sheet before the end! Promise?

OK let's get going. C'mon it will be fun!

1. When I am faced with fear, I:

   (a) Ignore it, trust my gut instinct and race ahead
   (b) Consult people I can trust, like family and friends, and then I make a decision
   (c) Consider worst and best case scenarios and make a decision accordingly

2. When one conceives the brand of their business or project, the first thing to think about is:

    (a) Make sure that my name and logo appeal to my target market
    (b) The reason for embarking on this business project in the first place
    (c) Name, logo, website, business cards, marketing collateral and brand colours

3. When I have an idea:

    (a) I first work out the practicalities and logistics to make sure it can be carried out
    (b) I mull it over at length to ensure it is the correct decision
    (c) If I instinctively think it's a great idea for business, I decide to do it first and work out the logistics later

4. When I embark on a new business or business project, I:

    (a) Go out there to meet as many people as I can to whom I could sell my products/services
    (b) Advertise (in magazines, radio, drop leaflets, etc.) to make as many people as possible aware of what I do
    (c) Look for opportunities to meet new contacts to tell them the story of my new project

5. Do you think outside the box?

    (a) What box?
    (b) No need to reinvent the wheel. There are tried and tested ways of doing things. The box is fine!
    (c) Easier said than done, it's not always practical

6. Do you have a 'dress down Friday' policy?

    (a) Yeah! It is always good to let your hair down at the end of the week

    (b) Every day is dress down Friday. As long as we look presentable when meeting customers, why should I care what I or anyone else wears while working?

    (c) No. To maintain our image and to ensure one is serious about business, I (and I believe others should) dress to impress every day

7. Do you send regular newsletters to update your contacts on what you have been up to since the last newsletter:

    (a) Religiously! I think it is very important to inform our customers about all the great things we do

    (b) Sometimes. I think it is worth sharing when something special happens in the business

    (c) Never! Why would they want to regularly read about us? People don't have time to read stuff like that

8. How many activities a year does your business engage with, that are truly different to those of your competitors?

    (a) Four or more

    (b) Two or three

    (c) One or none

9. If I'm lucky, then:

    (a) I am successful by chance or I was simply at the right place at the right time

    (b) 'Lucky shmucky', there is no such thing as luck. Any success I have is thanks to me

    (c) Me lucky? Doesn't happen very often unfortunately...

10. If I need a business lawyer, it most likely means:

(a) Oh boy... I'm in trouble!
(b) It's going to cost me...
(c) Good news!

Write your answers somewhere safe. You'll need them at the end. Patience is a virtue...

Chapter 1
It's Not About Timing

Time to make that dream come true!
This is the time you've been waiting for; the moment you've been dreaming about. It's your time to shine. You're now aware of your purpose; you feel your passion and are eager to set yourself free. You have identified the frustrations; you've even made a list and have ideas on how to begin resolving them. Exciting times!

Just a second, hold on, let me check my diary
But then you look at your diary and we lose you for good. It is so often at this exact moment we lose many who were set to join the revolution and be free. Right at the last moment, fear sets in again. Using the tools provided in part I, you have successfully overcome the initial fear that tried to stop you from thinking about following your dream altogether. But like a virus that mutates itself to a different form so it can overcome your medication, so does the fear creeping back in albeit in a different form. This time it is there dressed as an administrative advisor, a project manager, your business

advisor. It starts to tell you in its reprimanding tone that *'now is really not the right time!'* and then you repeat it out loud as an absolute truth.

It tells you in its serious reasoning manner that now is not the right time 'because the kids haven't started/finished school yet, because the renovation project of the house hasn't started/completed yet, because the market is a bit tough/strong/unpredictable at the moment; because mum/dad aren't feeling great and we need to see how things develop; because we have that big trip planned so let's reconvene after because 'this and that' must be sorted first *so let's take it from there'* (that's always a good one). And the list goes on. The fear now is all about timing, the only ammunition it has left in its war against you as you've overcome everything else. So it makes its final attempt to 'put some sense in to you' and says *'well if you're not going to listen to me and go ahead with that silly idea of yours anyway, at least wait! Wait until the time is right!'*

But guess what? It is rarely the 'right time'.

Timing isn't about your diary
There is never a right time to embark on your project or start your business. For example, I started writing this book at the worst possible time. Not deliberately, I hasten to add. I didn't go out there looking for the worst possible time. I had the idea of writing a book in my mind for a while, but it just happened that the inspiration to go ahead and do it came about when I was on an Ashram business trip to India. And there, the passion to write it was set alight. The purpose was clear, the revolution was happening all around me and I was meeting inspiring people along the way. But as far as my diary was concerned, it happened at the worst possible time.

It was the end of February and my firm was just approaching the end of its financial year. Our turnover had increased by 36% and profitability by 102%. This was fantastic news obviously, but it also meant it was the time when budgets had to be set for the following year and various financial discussions were being held that were very time consuming.

During this time I was also preparing for our big seventh annual **ACUMEN BUSINESS CONVENTION**, a prestigious event we organise ourselves with nearly 300 CEOs in attendance. Running alongside this I was busy working on our new website. To top these projects off, I had also embarked on a recruitment project for a marketing manager. Recruitment, as you are no doubt aware eats up your time. And I was also busy revamping our seven year old **ACUMEN** BUSINESS CLUB to something new and exciting, that no other usual networking chamber or club offers.

On the side, I also had five social media channels to run and an unprecedented busy period with legal work. All these new projects were over and above the usual hectic day to day activities of running the business, multiple marketing activities, legal work and of course having a family.

And then to top it all I decided I would start writing a book.

It made no sense! It would have been sensible and appropriate to wait until the new financial year's budget was complete, the new website was launched, the convention was over, the new club structure was complete and ready to launch and... we had our marketing manager in place, trained and able to help free up some of my time. By which point it would have been August when I had a few weeks booked to go away with the family. So I might as well have waited until that was over and start afresh in September, seven months later. Now that made sense. Of course it did. From a diary point of view, it was definitely the right thing to do.

Momentum is king!
But if I did wait until September, then, yes, all those projects would have been out of the way. But do you know what else would have been out of the way? The momentum, the energy and most likely the passion. I don't mean the momentum we create when we start doing something; I hadn't started writing the book so there was no 'book writing momentum'. I am referring to the momentum created inside you when that spark is ignited, passion is set alight and you feel out of this world, positive and buzzing with energy. You then have conversations that inspire you and suddenly you meet, read about and come across so many people and so many things that are relevant to your project that have not revealed themselves up to that point. Or so you think. They were there all the time of course, but your passion was turned off and there was no momentum, so you never saw them. In fact you would not have seen them had they stared you in the

face. But now they are present and visible and you are excited. You're dreaming again. It is this momentum I am referring to.

But you see the problem with momentum is that it is all about the now. Waiting is the momentum killer. It is impossible to quantify the importance of not losing momentum, but it can be the difference between following your dream or staying put with your frustrations.

Don't ever underestimate it.

Fear is the arch enemy of momentum
My fear was cunning. Not only did it apply the trick of 'you're way too busy it is just not the right time', but it also took the time threat one step further. It pointed out, sensibly of course, that as a very busy person I would never have time to write a book.

With fear you can sometimes overcome it or be defeated by it, but sometimes you can find yourself compromising because of it. That's what nearly happened to me. Instead of facing the fear and overcoming it, I found a compromise. I was going to engage a ghost writer to write the book for me! Eureka! By doing this I would not have to deal with the challenge of writing (tick off initial fear) and I would dedicate a lot less time (tick off the time fear). Sorted!

I am a great believer that when you make a genuine decision from the heart sparked by your passion, the universe conspires to make it happen. I have seen it happening again and again, on so many occasions and in relation to so many aspects of our lives. It happens almost like magic, or so it seems. You can't explain magic of course, but as a lawyer I am looking for facts and I have spotted a common theme.

When you truly and genuinely apply the liberating dictionary to your thoughts they turn into liberating and positive absolute truths in your life. Then if you coat these positive absolute truths with the high level energy you put out when you're passionately forging ahead with your new idea a momentum of some magnificence is created. At this point, you are in your element and are operating on a completely different level of consciousness. It is then that what seems like magic happens.

And that's what happened to me.

Just when I was about to give in to my fear and compromise, I met Dee Blick. Dee is a business woman, marketing ninja and a bestselling author of four business books. When I contacted her she suggested meeting for an afternoon cream tea and, book or no book, I never say no to a scone! When we met I told Dee about my passion to spread the Freedom Revolution so as many people as possible could join in and be free. I explained that I thought a book could be a fantastic tool to help achieve this and I shared my thoughts about taking on a ghost writer. Dee was adamant that my passion would best manifest itself with me writing it and not a third party such as a ghost writer. But being dominated by fear and its list of arguments, I was reluctant to agree with her.

But then, at the end of our meeting, Dee said: 'Go home and write your first chapter. It can be any chapter. Send it over. I will read it and share my thoughts with you. I won't charge you for it. I am passionate about you giving it a go yourself before deciding if a ghost writer is right for you. But I really want you to give it a go'. Well if you wanted an example of understanding the difference between an entrepreneur and an entreprewhore, there you have it. Dee was passionate about book writing and she was following her purpose and passion, the importance of income wasn't the prime driver for her. Dee wasn't pursuing a career as an author mentor and had rejected such requests in the past. But on this occasion she was passionate about me giving it a go. Dee subsequently became my paid author mentor, but none of us knew that at the time. Income came after, as it nearly always does. Dee was part of the revolution.

I took Dee's advice and I thought to myself there and then: I am going to go home and *start now! No more excuses!* We then set out to leave, but not before we had finished every crumb of that cream tea. Within a week I had written the first 5000 words. I was off.

This piece of advice is relevant to the starting of any project or business: '*Start it now. No more excuses!*'

The most important word of course is 'now'...

Because sometimes it really is now or never!
'Some people want it to happen, some wish it would happen, others make it happen' (Michael Jordan).

Make it happen.

Don't consult your diary for the perfect time. Whether it is perfect or not, has nothing to do with your diary. It has to do with your calling, as in literally when you are being called and the timing of you being called very rarely synchronises with your diary. When all the energy is channelled towards your passion and you feel that elated sense of purpose, a momentum is created. So whatever you do, don't miss out on it. It is a rare combination that doesn't manifest itself in our lives often enough. Had I decided after my cream tea with Dee to put my book writing project on hold for seven months because 'there is too much going on at the moment', that momentum would have dissipated and with it, most likely, the intensity of my passion. A lull would have followed and I can guarantee it would have been filled with fear, all the 'why nots' plus endless reasonable and sensible excuses. Fear would have triumphed again.

The same applies to my decision to set up the business. As I explained in part I it was the worst possible time for so many sensible reasons, commercial, economical as well as personal, but the momentum was there and the momentum prevailed! I went home and got started, there and then. No excuses.

So make a start **today**. Make that first step. Write down that first sentence. Make that first call. Look up that first matter. Do it. And do it now! No more excuses or procrastination!

Remember- what's the worst that can happen? Or even better, what's the *best* that can happen?!

Chapter 2
Brand! Brand! Brand!

Thriving on your passion financially

So there you are. You stared the fear in the face and successfully managed to overcome it. You got started. You used the momentum and took those vital first steps towards fulfilling your dream. You are getting on with it.

But at the moment it is still an idea. By 'getting on with it' I simply mean you have decided to give it a go. You're literally taking the first steps towards making your dream come true.

As I have shown, in the revolution profit follows passion and purpose. In the revolution era business people are thriving on their passion, but it is not an automated process. Being part of the revolution is a fundamental step towards enjoying financial success, as well as being free to pursue your passion. In the next pages I include practical tips to help you ensure that, as you are now part of the revolution, you can also thrive financially.

Brand for business is what location is for property
With property, they say that the first and most important thing to think about is the location. With your business one of the most important things to think about is your brand. The value of your brand is phenomenal. It is because of and thanks to your brand that someone makes a decision to work with you, collaborate with you, buy from you, talk about you, recommend you and pay for what you sell. It is not because of your price, your location or the number of people in your team. People buy from expensive providers, in unusual locations from one-person bands to multinational corporations. They choose you because of your brand and what it stands for.

What is a brand?
There are so many misconceptions in relation to a brand and what it really means. Often people think of a brand in terms of visuals: a logo, uniform, website, etc.

However a brand is first and foremost an emotional experience. An experience that is congruent with your business.

EasyJet and Rolls-Royce have different brands, not because they have different logo and colours but because they create different stories and different emotional experiences. Think of a business like a person. Daniel is so shy, Julie is committed and thorough, Zoe is outgoing and always the heart and soul of the party, Barry is untrustworthy and Jake is a bit old fashioned.

These are their 'brands'. What is yours? What do you want people to say about your business? 'Her business is....'? The words that will go in place of the three dots will be about your brand. People will remember the part of the experience that meant most to them for whatever reason. It may be that Daniel is shy but he is also very intelligent. But you mentioned he was shy because that was the experience that stuck with you the most, for whatever reason.

A pre-condition to the success of a brand
It cannot be emphasised enough how important stories are to your brand. Short, interesting and relevant stories about your business not only help define your brand, but they are also memorable and therefore can be

spread with ease by your groupies. Having a brand story that says you are good at what you do, is like telling you I can tell the time. It is seen as a given, unmemorable and not much of a 'story'.

If you and I met at a networking event and as we were sitting and having a coffee together you asked me what I do and I replied: '*I am from a firm of lawyers with two offices in the South. I am a solicitor that specialises in commercial law. For example I draft freelancers' agreements, terms of business, shareholders' agreements, website policies, NDAs and such other contracts. Sometimes I act for the business sometimes for...*' I am pretty confident I would have lost you at 'for example'! And even if you did listen politely to the bitter end, you would have mentally switched off and would most likely be thinking about what to have for dinner! Had someone asked you a week later who that person was that you had spoken to, I doubt you would have remembered our conversation let alone where I work and what I do.

But if I said: '*My name is Penina Shepherd and I am from* **ACUMEN** *BUSINESS LAW, an award winning modern law firm , probably different to most law firms you have worked with. Firstly we are business law specialists. So I won't get you divorced, well not today, or sort your home conveyancing, but I will take care of all the legal aspects of your business. We also have a unique charging system. We scrapped the hourly rate and we quote fixed fees at the outset for all non- contentious matters, so you can budget for them and always know where you stand. Last but not least is our culture and ethos. We have broken away from the aloof culture associated with our profession. We are approachable, accessible and unpretentious. We don't have secretaries, we do everything we possibly can electronically and are democratically run by all. If you see one of our lawyers in flip flops, don't worry it's one of the many ways we do happy. We care a lot about happiness. The FT listed us in the top 50 ground-breaking and innovative law firms in the whole of the UK & Europe, The Observer voted us a UK rising star and we have won many local awards.*'

Do you think you might be more interested? Is it a more memorable story?

Then, a fascinating thing happens when we see other people introducing us to someone we don't know. What you see happening is that they use our very own brand stories in their introduction. So, for example, it may be that one would say to another *'oh have you not met Penina? She is from Acumen; they have won lots of awards'*. Someone else might say *'they quote fixed fees'* and another *'they are top specialists in business law'* or *'you would love their energy, they are very different. Not your usual lawyers'* and so forth. Each person picks a different experience and part of the story that resonated with them, meant more to them or that was the most memorable to them. Because when a brand is memorable, it can be repeated thanks to the stories and emotional experiences behind it. You start the ball rolling by understanding that a brand is a story and an emotional experience and your marketing is the spreading of that story and experience.

The truth, the whole truth and nothing but the truth!
Your story has to be true! I know this is an obvious thing to say, but it is worth clarifying. It has to be true because it will very quickly become apparent if it isn't. Let's say Winterbottom & Sons Solicitors read this book and decide to 'adopt' Acumen's story, despite being a fuddy duddy law firm, it would never work. It wouldn't work even in less extreme examples. It is a short term strategy because when the client's actual experience whilst interacting with your business is not aligned with your brand, it creates a negative interaction. It is a disappointment. The story has to be aligned with who you truly are. People can change, stories can change, experiences can change, and so can your brand. But whatever you want it to be now, be sure to figure it out and express it in a short, interesting story. Then make sure the experience reflects the brand story.

Whilst your brand must be expressed in everything you say, it must also be expressed in everything you do. This is the vital part of 'your brand has to be true' conversation. If your lawyer introduces himself as innovative and mould breaking but when you go to meet him you are greeted by his secretary, taken to his office which has his name on the door (in case he forgets it!) and you find him resplendent behind a mahogany table, you naturally feel cheated. You feel the misalignment and it immediately creates a lack of trust. He is not what his brand story said his business was. Your brand creates an expectation and fulfilling that expectation builds that all important trust in you and your business. It also forms your groupies' community and their importance and influence is enormous.

Once I heard someone say 'pick your brand carefully'. However, if you join the revolution you walk in brand ready! It is your core; the passion and purpose that made you join the revolution in the first place. You have a burning desire to make a change so you can be free. And that is your brand. There is no brand for you 'to pick' and no story you have to invent. That 'burning desire to make a change so you can be free', **is** your story. You simply need to articulate it in all its glory so you inspire others to want to work with you and recommend you.

Communities

The relationships you create with your business communities can substantially enhance the value of your brand. Remember brands are about an emotional experience, so creating a community is a fantastic way to share experiences and emotions. Think about creating communities that are relevant to your business, even though on the face of it they might not directly benefit your business. For example, we set up the **ACUMEN** BUSINESS CLUB, an exclusive private club for businesses about business, not law. There was no guarantee any of the businesses would become clients, so there was no immediate answer to the 'what's in it for me?' question which is often asked in such a context. But there was an indirect answer in that it created a business community that was directly aligned to our brand. Of course many members did become our clients, and some already were. As I have said all along, follow your purpose and the income follows.

For the same reason we also set up the **ACUMEN** BUSINESS ACADEMY providing free legal and business seminars to businesses, **ACUMENTOR** - the Employers' Forum and **ACUMEDIA** a learning forum for the media sector. Each one had proved to be a great brand value asset.

Visuals

Just like everything else you say or do, your visuals must reflect your brand and not the other way round! It is no longer the case that your brand solely comprises of your visuals, that is your logo, website, banners, business cards and other marketing collateral. But the visuals are nevertheless a very important part of your brand. They must therefore reflect your brand so there is a clear, compelling and authentic connection between your story and the channels you use to communicate it. By way of example we felt that printed brochures did not reflect our brand so we don't have them.

At Acumen we do our best to make sure that every visual we use is aligned with our brand, our most prominent one being a zebra. Our logo is round, black and white with the zebra featuring in all our marketing. Out in the wild, all the four legged animals are either grey or brown, but suddenly this striking white horse appears, painted with black stripes, really standing out from the crowd; exactly what we wanted for Acumen. The idea behind the zebra fits with our core belief that we are not about fitting in but more about standing out. Black and white also fits well with law, because often people think the law is 'black and white' even though in reality it is a hundred shades of grey. But it works. We are constantly told our branding is very different, striking and fun.

Have fun with your brand
Business doesn't have to be serious all the time. When we launched our new offices at Gatwick we had a fabulous launch party, an opportunity to have fun with our brand. We had the launch event at a luxurious new Mercedes showroom. There was a free cocktail bar with barmen flying cocktails up in the air, fresh Italian food, a 'play your tune DJ', a photo booth, balloons and champagne. Whilst people were chatting and networking the background music fell silent and loud tribal drum music began to play. The two big showroom doors opened and twelve dancers in zebra tribal costume, faces painted emerged performing the most amazing flashmob dance. It was a truly spectacular event; a fun and lovely way to showcase our brand. People were talking about it for months after, even people who were not at the event but had simply heard about it. An invitation to a law firm's launch of a new branch strikes you immediately as an evening with wine, crisps and death by dull speeches. It doesn't have to be like that.

Be adventurous and playful with your brand. Think hard about how you can make it memorable for all the right reasons, making sure that what you decide to do is aligned with your brand.

And remember you are part of the revolution. Your brand already exists within you!

Chapter 3
Ginger Planning

Premise

Many people at this stage start by putting together a business plan. After all, this seems to be the first sensible thing to do as recommended by many business books and advisors. I talk about business plans later on, however, there is an initial step that comes before a business plan that cannot be skipped and yet that seems to be often overlooked. This is the exercise of setting out your **Premise**. Namely the foundation on which your idea, project or business will be built, figuring out what it is and writing it down. It doesn't have to be page after page of turgid text. It can be simple and concise, as long as you feel it genuinely sums up your Premise.

By way of an example, at my firm the Premise is divided to three sections:

(1) **ACUMEN** BUSINESS LAW - THE PEOPLE

The overriding culture is to:

1.1 have positive mindset & attitude;

1.2 treat each other with respect & dignity;

1.3 take full responsibility by each individual;

1.4 be extraordinary; and

1.5 enjoy the ride!

(2) **ACUMEN** BUSINESS LAW - THE CLIENTS

When interacting with clients we always strive to:

2.1 be remarkable;

2.2 provide systematic service;

2.3 recognise clients' wants when purchasing legal services;

2.4 be approachable, accessible and unpretentious; and

2.5 apply the highest standard to excellence.

(3) **ACUMEN** BUSINESS LAW - THE FIRM

The firm strives at all times to:

3.1 have respect for individuality;

3.2 ensure everyone must be able to influence (no hierarchy);

3.3 avoid the blame/fault culture;

3.4 contribute to the community and good causes;

3.5 thrive for and be proud of achieving prosperity & profitability.

Premise is all about the reasons why you joined the revolution in the first place, and it has to come first. Business Plans cannot be put together in isolation without the Premise as their foundation. Putting a Business Plan together without the Premise is likely to be as successful as a plan to start a diet on a Monday, it doesn't work. Imagine building a house without any drawn plans. Or, if your passion is to build an environmentally friendly, energy efficient house with a low carbon footprint. That is your Premise with regard to the house and any plan drawn subsequently will be entirely based on that passion, on that Premise. The drawn plan will be completely different to any drawn plan of a house that has none of these environmental concerns in mind. This is precisely the case when it comes to your project or business.

Ginger Business Plan

Business advisors may not like me for saying it, but Business Plans in their traditional format are little more than a dull, prototype, meaningless, exercise. Ditch them! They will be of no help whatsoever. The only time I prepared a Business Plan was when my bank forced me to do so. I found a template on the internet that had nothing to do with my business and I wrote the most BS it's possible to write down in a day. It was a box ticking exercise and it meant nothing.

Having said that, I do believe that writing a plan of the next steps you are going to take is important but it needs to be approached from a completely different point of view to the traditional Business Plan. It needs to be a completely different plan. Let's call it a Ginger Business Plan to differentiate it from the traditional ones.

The Ginger Business Plan is your Premise expanded.

Start by taking each part of your Premise and writing down how you are going to achieve it. Take into account and reflect in detail issues such as:

- Your industry related frustrations- what are they and how do you propose to resolve them?
- Competition - what do competitors do which is worth being inspired by and what are they missing?
- What could possibly hold you back and why?
- What could you be better at and how?
- Who could you collaborate with? What culture must they have and what values for you to work as complementary partners?
- Technology - are there technological features that could enhance your offering?
- What are the first five steps you must take?
- How much will it cost? Can you afford it or do you need to get finance? If you can't afford it and/or can't get finance, what would need changing?

Remember your Premise is your essence, core and passion. Expanding it will be a joy not a chore. That's the beauty of doing business in the revolution, because in the revolution your business is all about your essence, core and passion and that's why your business plan is a Ginger Business Plan. It is unique to you and your business. It is, literally, your dream plan and as such is like no other. There cannot be one standard template for a Business Plan for Winterbottom & Sons Solicitors that can also be used by **ACUMEN** BUSINESS LAW. I would hazard a guess that their Premise would be completely different to Acumen's, and therefore our Business Plan's instrument cannot be similar in any way shape or form.

Ginger Marketing Plan

There are two common mistakes in relation to marketing plans. The first one is the assumption that you set up a business first and put a marketing plan in place later on. This might have been correct outside the revolution, but in the revolution era the content of your marketing plan starts at conception! Your business DNA, your Premise, is your marketing plan. As a revolution business, you arrive with a built in marketing plan, a Ginger Marketing Plan!

You have to ensure you implement it by putting together the various strategies and tools to communicate your plan to your target market, and this is the second misconception. People confuse marketing plans with strategies. They are not synonymous. Marketing strategies are the tools to implement the marketing plan, and we will be discussing such strategies further on.

Whatever tools you select, your marketing plan should be summarised in two words: 'be remarkable'. Being remarkable is about being worth making a remark on. It is about being everything a thesaurus will tell you 'remarkable' is: extraordinary, amazing, notable, outstanding, noteworthy, significant, incredible and astonishing.

With your Ginger Marketing Plan, you will be all of these things.

The first thing you should do after reading this book is to read 'Purple Cow' by Seth Godin, if you haven't already. This book sets out beautifully what being remarkable is all about. But what is important to me here is to emphasise that a marketing plan is not a document that sits outside your business, alongside it or in parallel to it. The marketing plan is the implementation of your brand story and, as we discussed, your brand is the story of your essence.

If you joined the revolution, it is already in place. In the revolution it is so much easier to be remarkable. Do you know why? Remember in the first line of the first chapter of this book when I asked you: *"If money was no object I would...'* how would you complete this sentence? What would you do if money was no object in your business career?"* Well, in the revolution money is no longer the object. So all the things you said you could do if money was no object, you now can. You can be truly remarkable. What you need are the tools to tell the world about it. The moment you decided to give your dream a go, your marketing plan was already conceived.

In the revolution era, marketing is no longer *just* about your products or services it is about your Premise, your values. It is about the stories you use to tell the world about your passion and what you are doing to solve the frustrations and make them better.

So you faced the fear and made your decision. You ditched the excuses, took advantage of the momentum and made a start there and then. You have now set out your Premise, defined your brand and your Ginger Business & Marketing Plans have taken shape.

It is time to get to the office.

Part III

Wake Up and
Smell the Office

"You don't have to see the whole staircase,
just take the first step"
Martin Luther King

Chapter 1
The Due Date

Your first step
That's all you need to take now, just that first step. When you go on a 100 mile journey, all you see first is the end of your road. You cannot see the destination, you are nowhere near it. But you have just driven one mile, that's one mile nearer to your destination. You are, literally, on the journey.

Today is about your first mile, your first step. Today is the first day of making your dream come true. All the fears, hesitations, procrastinations, operational matters you had to resolve, various decisions you had to take, are behind you.

Today you have joined the revolution.

Be an entrepreneur not a worker

Your 'office' might be a spare bedroom, a shed, a small workshop, a table at a café or a desk space at the local co-working building. If you are a changemaker within a business, your 'office' may be your plan to start doing business internationally. Either way, you have arrived. You may have half a dozen clients/projects or 'leads' or you may, like me when I started, have none.

But that's ok because your 'job' during these early days has nothing to do with what you are skilled to do. You are now an entrepreneur. So if, for example, you are a web designer, an accountant, a gardener or a Head of Branch in an organisation, we take it as a given that you are a skilled worker. Your job at this point has nothing to do with your designing, accountancy, gardening or branch heading skills. It is all about being an entrepreneur, a FREE Entrepreneur. As we discussed in Part I, a FREE Entrepreneur is '*a creator and a changemaker in business who takes on reputational, emotional and financial risks to be free to pursue their passion and apply profit to make a positive impact on their life and other people's lives as a result*'.

Now is the time to take those risks. Your business idea might not work, your board might not like it, you could experience failure, you might lose money and your reputation could be tarnished. But you are an entrepreneur, and you desperately want to be a FREE one. You are doing it. It is you, the entrepreneur and not the skilled worker that has to turn up at the office on this first day.

One mistake commonly made by business people, is that they approach their business as technicians.[14] '*I am a carpenter; please come and buy tables and chairs from me*'. But why should I buy the tables and chairs from you and not from the many other carpenters in my town? The fact that you're a carpenter, a worker who can make tables and chairs, is a technician conversation. On your first day in the office you need to park your worker's skills aside, and engage in an entrepreneurial conversation.

The entrepreneurial conversation is about your passion. The reason you set out to be free in the first place. These are the conversations you should be having. Remember, your first day in the office is the day you go public. It is the day you start having those conversations with your community and potential groupies who don't even know you exist at this stage. It is the day you start planning the tools to implement your Ginger Marketing Plan.

I have a good idea!
When you are busy with your planning, you will come up with a few ideas. Do you remember the 'why not' arguments? Well they thrive now. Once you have an idea, often the first reaction is to tell yourself why your idea wouldn't work. Most of us are quite good at doing this.

The tactic of the 'why not' arguments when you have an idea, is to blind you with details. Say, for example, you had a great idea to run a road show of your products or services. The 'why not' will bombard you with a list of all the possible difficulties your idea creates: it will be difficult to get the right vehicle for that period of time; it will be a logistical nightmare to plan your accommodation along the way; you won't be able to have enough people with you on the road to provide the appropriate cover; it will be challenging to advertise your arrival in multiple locations; and the list goes on.

Like the arguments of fear, the 'why not' arguments are equally reasonable and convincing. But here it isn't about a major fear that paralyses you from doing something, but rather the practical side takes over your creative side and destroys it.

The worst thing is that sometimes ideas don't even get to see the light of day because they are thrashed by the details' brigade in your mind before you even said anything. What might be a fantastic idea comes up in your mind and then you get overwhelmed by the details and you think to yourself, 'no it just wouldn't work' and that's it, the idea is dead almost as soon as it was born.

More than half of the ideas I have come up with throughout the years have seemed implausible when the details were initially analysed. So when this happens ask yourself again, if details could be sorted is the idea a good idea? If the answer is yes, then do it. Make it happen. Solve the operational and technical details. Make it work. That's one of the reasons you are a changemaker, the fact that you can get past the details and make change happen. People with ideas are a ten a penny; people who follow the ideas up and implement them are scarce. Be that person. Bring up ideas. Overcome the operational details and follow them through.

Be a FREE Entrepreneur not a sales rep
Notice that I said "*Remember, your first day in the office is the day you go public. It is the day you start having those conversations with your community and potential groupies*", I didn't say it is the day you must start selling.

Now here is a bombshell! In the revolution you don't sell your products/ services, not to start with. In the beginning you don't sell anything. Google dictionary defines "selling" as '*give or hand over (something) in exchange for money*'. At this stage, unless specifically asked, you are not giving or handing over anything in exchange for money. You are spreading your passion. The more passionate you are about your purpose, the more committed you are about telling it, not selling it, then the more contagious it becomes.

You are here now to cause an epidemic.

"*Passion, intensity and tenacity. That's one way to describe Bill Gates. Bill Gates is a visionary that makes things happen, by creating systems bigger than himself and inspiring people to join him on epic adventures to change the world... He's a maker of impact.*"[15] As you can see, Bill Gates didn't go to 'the office' on his first day to sell software programmes. He sold a hell of a lot later on, but not at the initial stage. He was focused on one thing and one thing only, spreading his passion to change our lives by giving us tools that would empower us in a way unknown to mankind before. Mr Gates wasn't selling; he was making sure his passion was contagious thereby causing an epidemic.

Don't ever forget the reason why you joined the revolution in the first place. This is what it's all about. This is why you're going through everything you are at the moment. This is why people may engage you or work with you. This is your brand. This is your Ginger Marketing Plan. Don't spoil it by shifting the conversation from your passion to make things better to a selling conversation. Not just yet. The sales will come. Be patient, although being patient doesn't mean sitting still and doing nothing; not at all.

Be shameless
So this is it! Your baby is ready to be delivered. The contractions are every few minutes. It is about to happen any time now.

"I gave birth quietly just whispering" said no woman ever!

The baby is ready to come out. It's time to scream your heart out. It is time to tell the whole world about it!

'Screaming' about your new business doesn't mean spamming, interrupting, intruding and 'in your face' selling and promoting. 'Screaming' is about engaging with your relevant community in an interesting and captivating manner. It is time for all of them to hear about your passion.

It is time to tell the tale.

Holding a launch party can be the first step in shamelessly telling everyone about it. Invite the members of the local chamber of commerce organisations and of course your existing contacts. But you must put on an interesting event. For you of course this is a life changing event but for everyone else it's just another networking event in their diary. What could make your event stick out? Revisit the discussion we had in part II 'In a World of Black & White, Be Ginger' and be remarkable because it applies to everything your business will be doing and this includes your very first event. Most businesses do the standard stuff. Standard is mediocre. It has no colour and, as we said, in a world of black & white, add some colour and be ginger! Stand out with your lovely fire colour hair and your beautiful freckles. Be remarkable. Make your event one that attendees will talk about when they return home to their partner or back to the office to their colleagues.

When planning your event consider 'what's in it' for your guests much more than 'what's in it for you'. What will be so great about your launch event for them? Why wouldn't *they* want to miss it?

The event doesn't have to be expensive. When I started **ACUMEN** BUSINESS LAW, I teamed up with four other business people, specialists in marketing, IT, HR and finance. We set up a group company **ACUMEN** BUSINESS GROUP offering these five disciplines and together we rented a two storey office. We had a wonderful launch party there. In the weekend beforehand we painted the boardroom making it as nice as we could on our limited budget and using our own resources. For the party, we hired a grand piano and placed it in the boardroom (it had to be delivered in through the windows!). We invited a local but nationally known entrepreneur who told his amazing business story. We invited all the local press and of course, provided food and drinks. Each one of us invited business people we knew. It was a blast on a very limited budget. We got a two page spread in the business section of the local paper and many business magazines in the area reported on it. We didn't pay for any of this coverage. They were intrigued by the story of five disciplines joining together.

What story can you create that will be of interest to your local media and business community? What will your launch event look like? What will be different about it? What's in it for the attendees? Why should they bother? Be creative. Be remarkable. Be shameless and tell everyone about it.

Chapter 2
Pioneer Groupies

They love you!

If you are in the revolution seeking freedom, I can tell you straight away that your target market isn't everyone with a pulse and a purse/wallet. In fact, it is quite the opposite. It's not about you *'can't* win them all' but is rather that you *'don't want* to win them all'. You want to limit your target market to the groupies of your community, certainly at the first stage.

The 'pioneer groupies' are the very first followers within your potential larger groupie community. They are the people who share your passion and love what you do. They get it. They get you. And they are the first ones to embrace it. Let's say for example that your business sells environmentally friendly pens. If I don't particularly care about the environment or am neutral about it, there's little point trying to sell your pens to me, definitely not at the beginning. I will not be one of your pioneer groupies. However, if I am passionate about the environment then I will be the kind of person who reads articles about it, 'likes' relevant environmental pages on Facebook and follows such people on Twitter. I will be a keen recycler and will be counting my footprint as though they were sleeps before Christmas. I am your perfect potential groupie. I will absolutely love your environmentally friendly pens and will be very likely to buy them and recommend them to likeminded people in my community. So, in this instance, it is people who are passionate about your passion who will be your pioneer groupies.

However your pioneer groupies don't necessarily have to share your passion. They can become your very first followers because they love your new approach. By definition, pioneers are people who love trying new things. They love new ideas and finding different ways of going about doing things. Challenging the status quo isn't a discomfort for them, quite the opposite in fact. If the business community was a class on a school trip, they'd be the cool guys at the back of the bus.

It is precisely these types of people who formed Acumen's pioneer groupies. They were not people who were passionate about the manner in which legal services were provided (funnily enough...), but they were people who loved our new approach. 'Acumen is like a breath of fresh air' they would tell us. They were up and coming modern businesses, established as well as start-ups. Quite a few were from the digital media sector in which they were being revolutionary themselves. They were proud of us, even admired us for the fact that we dared challenge such a long established tradition and profession. And like all pioneer groupies who love what they see, they wanted to be part of it. They were proud to be part of it and felt a great sense of connection to a group whose culture and values aligned perfectly with theirs. And if you don't believe me just see what happens when one VW Campervan sees another VW Campervan coming in the opposite direction.

The beauty about working with the pioneer groupies is that they don't just become your customers, they also, by definition, become your fans. They are your raving fans and they create a fan club community by passionately talking about you. They become your best sales force and they are doing it of their own accord.

Rearguards

Rearguards are the opposite of pioneer groupies. Rearguards are the people who will only work with a business if it is well established and there is evidence of their previous work. If they see a sign saying 'here since 1923', it's poetry to their ears. For the pioneer groupies words such as 'established' and 'here since 1923' can sometimes read as 'old fashioned', 'stuck in their ways' and 'lacking innovation', but for the rearguards it reads 'safe', 'secure' and 'settled'. Words such as 'new' and 'different' terrify the rearguards.

But the fantastic news is that the people in the middle, those standing between the pioneer groupies and the rearguards, and sometimes even some of the rearguards themselves, eventually join in too. Many of them eventually start to follow the pioneer groupies. They feel that the concept is no longer new (which for them means risky), but it is now 'tried and tested' and the cool guys seem to love it. So they want to be part of it too.

Each and every one of us can sometimes be a pioneer groupie with regard to some matters and a rearguard with regard to others. I remember when I upgraded my Sony Ericsson mobile phone to the first touch screen iPhone. I hated it! It always seemed I touched the wrong thing and everything I tried to do wasn't working. I remember saying, 'I think I will go back to my good old Sony Ericsson. It was perfect. I hate this new thing'. I was definitely a rearguard in this instance, or maybe one of those standing in the middle as I was at least willing to give it a go. But I was certainly not a pioneer groupie. I didn't want it. I was dragged into it kicking and screaming by wanting to be part of the cool guys with this new touch screen gadget. But as I sit and type these lines I have the latest edition of the iPhone to my right and a new iPad to my left. I clearly followed the pioneer groupies. I joined in. I came round. If Apple aimed their marketing strategies at me and people like me on day one, they wouldn't be where they are today. But they didn't. They aimed it at their pioneer groupies; at those people who always know exactly when the new Apple product is about to launch, who study its features intently and queue all night so they can be first in line to have it on launch day. Then as long as there is a good brand story and the product/service is aligned with the brand promise, the others just follow suit; even the rearguards.

As I mentioned, when Acumen was set up, it was the pioneer groupies who began interacting with us first and became our fans. But then, a little later, the groupies in the middle started to interact with us too. They saw the pioneer groupies doing it and they followed suit. And now businesses within the rearguard community comfortably work with us. We remain different and mould breaking for the pioneer groupies, but tried and tested enough to put the rearguards' mind at rest.

We will be discussing the available marketing strategies that will help you find and interact with your pioneer groupies in Chapter 4 of this Part. But for now, ask yourself:

- Who are your pioneer groupies?
- Where can you find people who are passionate about your passion?
- What type of people would welcome your new initiative?
- How should you interact with them so that it is aligned with your purpose and theirs?
- What could you say that will be music to their ears?

If you can answer these questions and follow them up with your actions then you will have a pioneer groupies' community around you as your fans and you are going to be, well, ginger in a world of black & white.

In the revolution all relationships are consensual
When the entreprewhores set up in business they have to come up with a complete marketing plan on their first day in the office. There is no passion or purpose, but only the pursuit of profit. So their marketing plan is to find as many people as possible with a pulse and a purse/wallet who will buy from them. They often have to engage in 'cold calling' tactics and, therefore, operate in hostile conditions.

As a FREE Entrepreneur you are in a much more privileged position, while still ending up making no less profit than the entreprewhore. Firstly, as we discussed in Part II, you arrive at your first day in the office with your marketing plan built in, that is your essence, your passion and your purpose. Then you had to spend a little time polishing and refining it in your written Premise and deciding on the tools and strategy to implement it. Secondly, as you are in pursuit of passion and freedom rather than just profit, your focus will be on meaningful engagement with the right members of the community where your passion is most likely to become contagious. It is the community where your pioneer groupies are waiting for people just like you to carry the flag of your common purpose. Therefore, unlike the entreprewhore, you will be engaging in a consenting environment and will be able to have consenting marketing relationships.

But will they let you in?

Chapter 3
St Peter and the Pearly Gates

St Peter is semi-retired

The Pearly Gates of heaven are guarded by St Peter. St Peter isn't just any old guard. He is the keeper of the *keys to the kingdom* and those who, in his eyes, are not fit to enter heaven, are denied entrance at the gates and descend into hell.

The world is full of St Peters. They are the people who decide if you get the job, if your business news will be advertised in the local paper, if your book will be published. They hold the keys to our desired kingdom and if we (in their eyes only) are not deemed fit to enter our desired place, our heaven, they shut the gates in our face and we go to hell. We have all been at those Pearly Gates wondering how St Peter of our world would feel about us. Would he let us in?

Well I am the bearer of good news.

St Peter is now semi-retired. He only works part time these days. He only works a few hours a day, a few days a week. The rest of the time the keys to the kingdom are held by you.

Yes, that's right, by you.

The internet pulled the rug from under St Peter's feet. Before the internet, the only way for me to publish this book for example would have been to tirelessly approach, more likely beg, publishers until one St Peter publisher opened the kingdom gates for me and allowed me in. Or, they wouldn't and then both me and my book dream would tumble to hell. Similarly, before the internet, you had to have a personal connection or 'pull some strings' with your local newspaper editors for them to publish a feature about you or an article you wrote.

With the internet, which obviously includes emails and social media, we all hold the keys. We don't need St Peter's permission anymore. We can pave our way to heaven via the Pearly Gates. We can write our own blogs and publish them on our website and on other relevant forums; we can publish our own magazine if we want to. Before emails we had to incur huge expense in printing and postage. We don't anymore. We can reach millions of people at a press of a button. Your cat can be viewed online by millions of people worldwide and all it has to do is be scared of a cucumber. St Peter would not have allowed that!

This is tremendously empowering.

Think about it. You were handed the keys! So what are you going to do about it?

As Spiderman will tell you, with power comes great responsibility, and that's from a man who climbs walls for a living! You now have this immense power so you can no longer hide behind St Peter. You no longer have to wait for the St Peters of the world to show you in. You have to *get in there*. You must be active. It is all down to you now.

How does that make you feel? Does it scare you or empower you? Remember the mindset conversation in Part I? Now is a good time to use what you learned there. Make sure you approach it with the right mindset and the right dictionary. No negative sinking into fear. These are the keys to the gates of the kingdom…to your heaven.

So what are you waiting for? Go down there now and open those gates. It is St Peter's day off.

Chapter 4
Revolution Marketing Strategies

So much is already in place

When you 'woke up and smelt the office', so much was already in place. Firstly you arrived at the office with your marketing plan already built in. You then went about conducting yourself as a FREE Entrepreneur and not as a skilled worker. It was all about spreading the passion via your stories, not about selling your skills because as a FREE Entrepreneur, you wouldn't engage with people as a sales rep at this stage. You may have had a fabulous launch party that was well attended. You then focused on spreading your passion and were aiming at your pioneer groupies ready to have consensual marketing relationships with them. You then arrived at the Pearly Gates and were given the keys. You are in!

Now that's not a bad start!

You are now comfortably in the kingdom, the gates closing behind you. It's time to start marketing your business. As we said you are focusing on spreading the passion so you need to find your pioneer groupies and, to do that, you need marketing strategies that will implement your Ginger Marketing Plan. Not just any old marketing strategies, but revolutionary ones.

As you will see the actual strategies I am recommending are not new, it is the manner in which you implement them that is different. Therefore, whichever tools you decide to adopt, please remember this one important rule: it is a black & white world out there. Most do the standard stuff. Standard is mediocre. Stand out. Be ginger!

Networking

'People buy people' as the saying goes and it is true. Even if you are engaging with a large corporation, your decision to buy from them or not may be determined by the call centre rep who took your call and if you 'bought' the rep you were more likely to buy the product.

But you most likely 'bought' the brand to start with. It may be that you 'buy' Virgin's services because you 'bought' its unique brand story spearheaded by Richard Branson or that you buy Body Shop products because you 'bought' the environmental story spearheaded by Anita Roddick. So yes, people definitely buy people, but people, as we established above, also buy brands and brands are emotional experiences and the stories we use to convey them.

Networking is the ideal place where people, brands and their stories can spread.

Indeed one of the best ways to get people to know you and your story is by networking. Join your local chamber and explore other networking organisations in your area. Do the 'leg work'. Digital networking is great too, something I mention later in this chapter, but nothing replaces the energy that is transmitted between two people in a face to face meeting. It will be in these networking events that you start identifying your potential groupies and begin building relationships with them.

The essence of networking is creating relationships, not selling. How can it be about selling? Think about it, how many times have you attended a networking event thinking 'today I am going to go to a networking event to buy some services'? I am guessing not many. Rarely does anyone attend an event with an intention to buy, so why would you attend an event with an intention to sell? Would you like it if a delegate approached you at a networking event and tried to hard sell you their products or services? With time, everyone gets to know who these people are and eye contact with them is avoided at all costs.

However, please don't turn my advice on its head whereby you are so terrified about coming across as 'salesy' that you don't even tell people what it is that you do. This is just as bad. You are there to get to know people and to introduce yourself too.

Having said that networking is a great way to get people to know you and your story, it cannot and must not ever be *just about* getting to know you and hearing *your story*. A mistake some people make when they go networking is to be completely focused on themselves. They are only interested in telling you *about them* and have no interest in listening to you talking about you and your business. I have been in conversations when the other person was talking about their business fully engaging, but as soon as it was my turn to talk their eyes were scanning the room planning who they could talk to next about themselves. Don't be that person. Networking is all about creating relationships and to do this you must engage with the other person and with their story. Being self focused is not only a fruitless business approach, it is also rude and no one likes engaging with rude people.

Relationship building entails a two way interaction. Engage, listen, and show that you are listening by making relevant comments or asking related questions. Then, when the time is right, you can comfortably bring the conversation to you and what you do. As discussed in Part II, please ensure your story is interesting, memorable, different and engaging.

Now here's my most important tip about networking: make sure that your interesting, memorable, different and engaging brand story can be told in 90 seconds. Write it down and memorise it off by heart as if you are about to perform it in a play. Why? Because these 90 seconds will form the core of your brand story from now until the end of time, well the rest of your business life at least. If you attend events where you stand up and introduce yourself, you will have your 90 seconds ready. If you have a casual conversation by the coffee table at an event, you can use your 90 seconds or refer to some of it. If you have a 1-2-1 networking lunch/coffee meeting, you can take your 90 seconds and expand on it. When you start recruiting people, you will be able to use the slightly expanded 90 seconds to introduce the business to them and if and when they join, they too will have a punchy summary of the brand story in their armoury.

At **ACUMEN** BUSINESS LAW we always recommend that our new recruits attend speed networking events. This way they get to repeat the 90 seconds story, the one I laid out in Part II, time and time again so that by the end of the event they know it off by heart. If speed networking events take place in your area be sure to attend them and go armed with your fabulous 90 seconds story.

And don't be shy or scared about being shameless! Everyone is at a networking event for the same reason. If a person was queuing in the supermarket and you approached her and started telling her all about you and your business and asking questions about her, well she may well call security. But what is clearly odd behaviour in this scenario is perfectly normal and acceptable at a networking event. Most people attend events on their own and are there for the same reason as you. It would not be frowned upon if for example I approached a person hand outstretched and said with a smile 'Nice to meet you I am Penina Shepherd from **ACUMEN** BUSINESS LAW, where are you from?' And let the conversation flow from there.

Beware of a common networking trap too. We are all instinctively drawn to people we know and you may end up only ever talking to the same people that you already know. It is important to clarify that not only is it absolutely fine to approach and speak to people you already know at networking events, but that in fact you should. This is how you forge relationships by catching up with people more than once. Business reasons aside, it would be rude to ignore them, and that certainly won't help in forging relationships with them. But, after a few minutes and at the right time, you can confidently bring the conversation to an end saying something along the lines of "It was really good catching up with you.

Good luck with xyz" (showing you were actually listening) and then move on. If you are 'stuck' with people who will not 'let you' leave, then 'I am off to get a drink', 'grab a sandwich' or 'to the loo' are always handy things to say without causing offence as you move on.

Using the St Peter principle, don't just wait to be invited by others to what you would regard as the perfect networking event. Why not create that perfect event yourself? It may be workshops, seminars, parties, etc. Our **ACUMEN** BUSINESS CLUB, **ACUMEN** BUSINESS CONVENTION, **ACUMEN** BUSINESS ACADEMY, Acumedia have all proven to be great networking events for us and we set up some of those when we were only one year old.

Of course, all of this takes time, often huge amounts of it. But I don't remember promising you an easy ride anywhere in the book. I promised you that if you are in the revolution following your passion you will be loving what you do but nevertheless you have to invest the time. At Acumen, not only have we invested time in creating our own events, we also remain consistent. Once conceived, we carried on delivering them without fail. It is not an easy task, but it is worth it. Your business is worth it.

Digital marketing

When it comes to digital networking, there are many experts on social media platforms who will advise you on how to grow your following as well as provide you with SEO and technical advice.

I am not a digital expert, but what I can say from experience is that many of the offline networking principles apply to online networking. If you have a Twitter account but never tweet, it is like going to a networking event, standing in the corner and not talking to anyone. If you post Facebook posts just about yourself, but never interact with other people's posts then you are like the person at a networking event who is only interested in talking but not listening. If your social media profile is dull and standard, it is like having a dull and standard 90 seconds intro.

An important digital marketing strategy to consider is videos. Videos are huge in this digital era. We have our own Acumen YouTube channel where we upload numerous videos. I have personally recorded two series so far of 'Penina's Perspective On:... ' whereby each video in the series is about a different topic (e.g. trademarks, intellectual property, shareholders' agreement, etc.).[16] The most important thing is to make sure the videos are short. All my videos are three to five minutes long. They can of course be shorter.

How can you use videos to tell your story or showcase what you are offering and why it is remarkable? Are there any short videos you can put together that will be helpful to your groupies?

Collaboration

We are stronger together. So, consider aligning yourself with others as mutual collaborators. It is a mistake to think of your 'target market' as just your potential customers. Your target market is also comprised of your potential referrers; those people who also work with your target market and could refer work to you and vice versa. Identify them. Could you run marketing events together? Could you write blogs for their website and vice versa on complementary and not competing topics? Could you arrange monthly or quarterly meetings where you can inspire and be inspired?

The important thing to consider is who you should get into bed with. For example:

- Do they get your dream and do you get theirs?
- Can you inspire, and be inspired by, them?
- Can you happily connect them with others?
- Would your groupies like them?
- Is their brand aligned with yours?
- Do your culture and values complement each other?

As collaborators they will be seen as an extension of you so you don't want to be damned by association. But once you collaborate with the right people, it can be incredibly powerful.

Mailshots - ditch the newsletter!

Mailshots are a great marketing communication tool and in this digital era, much of the interaction is indeed via emails. Newsletter mailshots, on the other hand, are the worst kind. Scrap them! Newsletters are always about the sender: '*Look at what we have been up to this month at our company*' shout so many newsletter headlines.

No one cares!

Not wanting to sound harsh, but no one cares what my business has been up to this month. The fact that Jane the book keeper has joined us might be scintillating news for us, but is of absolutely no interest to you. The fact that I ran a seminar with 35 people is of great interest to my mum but alas not enough for the web designer down the road to interrupt her busy day. The fact that we went on a team building trip and Simon fell in the water is hilarious to us but for others…well… I guess they had to be there, but they weren't so they don't care!

At **ACUMEN** BUSINESS LAW all our mailshots are without fail about the recipient. It may be an invitation to an event, a legal tip, some information about a change in the law, a blog with material that can be relevant to the recipient's business, etc. Even when I was invited to 10 Downing Street to represent small and medium size businesses, we sent a mailshot asking recipients if there was anything they wanted me to ask on their behalf. Of course these mailshots do enable us to tell you about us too. Through these mailshots you get to learn that we organise seminars, specialise in the subject you received a legal tip on and that we are sufficiently influential in the business community to be invited to 10 Downing Street, etc. But the unstinting focus of the mailshots is you. Invite *you*, educate *you* and represent *you*, unlike newsletters that are all about the sender.

So ditch the newsletters. Replace them with engaging communication tools that appeal to the recipient because the message is all about *them*.

Marketing collateral
Your marketing collateral is the equivalent of you holding up a mirror for all to see you. It is the image of your business. It must therefore be completely aligned to your brand story; a perfect reflection of it as it forms an important part of your image.

Marketing collateral comprises your website, letters, business cards, emails, banners, brochures and leaflets (digital or printed), uniform, videos; even your Premise. Anything physical that represents your business is part of your marketing collateral. It must be a mirror image of your business story.

So if your business story is about being prestigious, exclusive and premium, don't use cheap DIY Word design. If your business story is about the environment, use recycled paper. If your business story is that you are established, safe and traditional, your colours will most likely be in safe colour shades of blue and grey with symmetric shapes. If your brand story is that you are mould breaking, innovative and different, then your colours may be warm and welcoming 'yorange' with some crazy black & white zebras dotted around.

During the process of establishing your marketing collateral you may find yourself in a meeting trying to decide which design to select for it. The conversation may well be along the lines of 'oh wow I really like this one' or 'I really don't like that one'. However, when it comes to your marketing collateral, it is not about what you like, it is about whether it is aligned with your brand story and relevant to your target market. You may see a cheap futon and say 'wow I really like that', but then it may look totally out of place in your contemporary marbled penthouse apartment.

When the marketing collateral is not aligned with your brand story there is a breach of trust. It is just as I mentioned in Chapter 2 of Part II. If your lawyer introduces himself to you as innovative and mould breaking but when you meet him you are greeted by his secretary and it all feels very stuffy with a mahogany desk, name plate on the door and the like, you naturally feel cheated. You feel the misalignment and it immediately creates a lack of trust. He is not what his brand said he was.

This is precisely the case with your marketing collateral. It has to accurately reflect your brand story.

Build your database
From day one you have to build your database. Every single person you come into contact with in your business circle, add them to your database. It will become one of your most precious assets with time.

Always ask for a business card at a networking event. Anyone that contacts you by email, add them to your list. Any enquiry you receive, whether it converts into business or not, add to your list. Then the next time you organise an event or send a professional tip, these people are on your list. You are keeping in touch. Otherwise you may never see some of these people again and could miss an opportunity to forge relationships with them in the future.

Public speaking

Public speaking is another great marketing strategy tool. It gives you a fantastic opportunity to engage with many people with all the attention and focus on you. But you must not abuse it. If you abuse the fact that you have a captive audience and try to use it as a sales pitch instead, then you will not be invited to give a talk again and your talk will not achieve the positive impact you were hoping for.

There are plenty of experts who run courses on public speaking. I have never attended one myself but if public speaking doesn't come naturally to you it is probably a good idea to attend one.

My top tips with regard to public speaking are:

- If your talk is on something that you are passionate and knowledgeable about, you don't need a huge amount of preparation.

- Do not read from notes. Very few things are more boring than watching someone else reading on the stage. It is up there with watching paint dry.

- Be animated, it shows you are talking about an engaging topic that you are passionate about.

- Don't put your hands in your pocket and play with your keys/change (men).

- Don't paste chapter and verse of war and peace on your slides. It causes depression; it just hasn't been proven yet.

- Use anecdotes, case studies, real stories as these bring your presentation to life.

- If the topic allows, and nearly all topics do, even the most sombre ones, be humorous.

- Make your presentation about the audience not about you. So if your talk is about your business journey, relate it to the audience. If it is about educating the audience about a topic that you are an expert in, relate the topic to their businesses.

Awards

Business awards are a marketing tool definitely worth considering, especially for a new business or project. Once you have this formal recognition, your new business or project will have more clout and authority.

Awards are of less significance for the pioneer groupies' community because, by nature, they are not seeking third party validation. They prefer to 'live on the edge' and try new things themselves, as long as they share your passion and are aligned with your core values which, if they are your pioneer groupies, they will be by definition. But for those communities who sit behind the pioneer groupies, and certainly for the businesses in the rearguards' community, they find great comfort in knowing that you have won awards. It gives them the feeling of confidence that you have been scrutinised and approved by a third party and therefore it is less risky to interact with you.

For established businesses, awards are also a great PR tool. They give you publicity in local publications, an opportunity to network at the event itself and a nice award to put on the shelf for all to see.

Geographical stretch

If you have an online business, then of course you can work with businesses anywhere in the world. If you are a freelancer working as a cleaner, then you have to work in relative proximity to your home as it will make no sense to drive to the other side of the county for a cleaning assignment on a daily or weekly basis.

But what if you are neither? What if you are a local business selling products or services to your local community? Could you not sell your products or services further afield?

ACUMEN BUSINESS LAW is a Brighton and Gatwick based firm and whilst we work with many businesses in Sussex, we work with businesses from all over the Uk and abroad. We use technology, or as we internally refer to 'Legal FaceTime', which enables us to do this. Don't be limited by the belief that you can only serve your local community. Since the internet entered our lives, the world is truly a small village. As we say on our website: *'Too far for a meeting? Absolutely fine, we can do Legal FaceTime anywhere anytime'.* And so can you.

Ad hoc strategies

Ongoing strategies aside, it always pays to consider good reasons for ad hoc strategies. For example when we launched our new office at Gatwick, the launch party we had wasn't part of our ongoing strategy of course. It was an ad hoc one off strategy. Ad hoc strategies can include celebrations, although I am always careful about holding company birthday parties. Again, it is one of those examples where you are excited about a significant company landmark, but the fact you are three or seven or even twenty years old, is of little importance to anyone else. But, if you can use your birthday as an excuse for a great ginger party, then absolutely, go for it.

Always have your eyes open looking for the right opportunity for a remarkable marketing strategy that will assist in telling everyone your brand story.

Innovation

ACUMEN BUSINESS LAW was listed by the Financial Times in the top 50 ground-breaking and innovative law firms in the whole of the UK and Europe. The reason I am mentioning this again, (apart from because I really want to...) is to stress that innovation doesn't have to be about technology. When we were listed we had no technological innovations whatsoever. But we innovated in everything we did, and still do.

I set out our innovative offering in Part I and our innovative brand in Part II. You will see in Part IV that we also innovated internally. Similarly in this part III, innovation finds its way in our marketing. The often repeated sentence in this book, 'in the world of black & white, be ginger', is my way of saying: make sure you always innovate. Think of new ideas as well as new ways of approaching existing ideas. Do something that it is worth remarking on.

Giving

Finally I want you to think about giving. Now this is an unusual strategy for a lawyer! Have an open door policy and a mindset to help when you can. Reach out to people and when possible, help them out.

Make sure that every year your business engages with at least one charity. Every year we use the fantastic platform of our **ACUMEN** BUSINESS CONVENTION to promote a charity. We give them a stand and promote them on stage and in all the event related marketing collateral. They get the same deal as our head sponsor, obviously at no cost.

I have included 'Giving' in this section because it can absolutely form a marketing strategy. But it is an odd one. It is the only strategy I wouldn't recommend measuring your return on investment. Just give for the sake of giving, if you don't get anything out of it, you will still feel great and you will have helped a great cause. One day, someone will help you, but don't keep score.

Whichever marketing strategy you apply, please do remember the golden rule: in a world of black & white, be ginger!

Part IV

You're Free!

"Everything that is really great and inspiring
is created by the individual who
can labour in freedom"

Albert Einstein

Chapter 1
You Are Living the Dream

Freedom

This is it. You're living the dream. When you 'woke up and smelt the office' you officially joined the revolution. You are now in full momentum and are giving it your all. This is all you can think about and, if you could, this is all you would talk about to anyone who would listen. You're constantly thinking of new ideas, when you are driving, showering, eating or just about to fall asleep. You are literally living and breathing it. You're consumed within it. The notion of 'Sunday night blues' makes no sense at all. Sometimes you are a bit frustrated by the delays caused by the weekends, although you might not admit it aloud so as not to be judged. The whole 'is it business or is it pleasure?' conversation is irrelevant, as the line between when business ends and pleasure starts is completely blurred.

You are immersed with the sense of freedom all around you. At last you are no longer simply fantasising about your purpose, you're pursuing it full steam ahead. You can now truly start to feel that you are aligned with your passion and core values. And you're experiencing the most incredible euphoria. You are in the now and full of consciousness. You feel alive. Freedom has outplayed fear and now what you think, what you say and what you do are in harmony. You are truly happy.

This is what it feels like to be free.

It's time to live the dream. Should we wish you all the best of luck?

Luck

You will hear many people wishing you good luck. Well I am here to share a secret with you. The vital secret of how luck is brought about into your life; into all aspects of your life, business life as well as personal. What is luck? Let's go back to the dictionary:

> 'Luck is success or failure apparently brought by chance rather than through one's own actions.'

Wrong.

I would argue that the exact opposite is correct and that luck actually is:

> "Success or failure **not** brought by chance, **but rather** through one's own actions."

I would go one step further and support the statement that "there is no such thing as luck; there is only adequate or inadequate preparation to cope with a statistical universe"[17]

Whether you are lucky or not depends on your 'adequate or inadequate preparation to cope with a statistical universe'. What does 'statistical universe' mean, I hear you ask.

It means opportunities. And your life is full of opportunities...

All the time.
Every day.
Today.
Right now.

It is possible that reading this book at this very moment will turn out to be an opportunity for something. It could make you take a step that leads you to a successful outcome you wouldn't otherwise have thought of. So by reading this book you are increasing your universe statistics 'to be lucky', as opposed to others who haven't. By regularly attending networking events, to use another example, you are *adequately* prepared for the opportunities they can generate. By taking an action and attending them you are increasing your universe statistics 'to be lucky', as opposed to those who don't regularly attend networking events.

The crucial thing to understand is that luck is not a passive event that happens to you. Luck is the actions you take and your reactions to events. In fact luck is the result of four main actions:

- Thinking positively (70,000 thoughts! Remember?)
- Learning
- Keeping an open mind
- Acting

If you think positively, learn, keep an open mind and act you will be adequately prepared for when the universe statistics reach you!

You will be lucky.

The NME online magazine published an article entitled: *'Paul McCartney says he was 'flattered' and 'lucky' to work with Kanye West'*.[18] McCartney said he felt 'lucky'. But was he lucky in the dictionary meaning of the word? Was the fact he was working with Kanye West brought about by chance as per the dictionary definition or was it through McCartney's own actions as per the definition I have suggested?

Well look at what Mr McCartney said further down in the same article: "*It's good to connect with different artists...The secret is I keep myself very open to suggestions - I still feel like I'm about 30.*" It seems that Mr McCartney knows the secret I am sharing here too. He keeps himself open to suggestions and he feels he is 30. In other words what he is saying is that he thinks positively (he thinks he is 30... he's not but that's how positive he is!), he is always learning (rapping is certainly not his usual genre), he keeps an open mind (as he said so himself) and he acts upon it. No wonder he feels lucky. He followed the four steps and substantially increased his universe statistics.

What you will find is the more actions you take, the more you increase your universe statistics. The more trees you shake, the more fruit will fall. The more you are in the 'doing', the more lucky you will become. Professor Philippe Gabilliet put it beautifully: "*Luck isn't found in what happens, but in what you do with what happened. Luck is not an event, but rather how you react to an event.*"[19]

Flip it on its head. Think about the so called 'unlucky people'. How many times was an opportunity staring them in the face and they didn't see it? When does it happen? It happens when people are off guard; when people go into negative sinking; when many of their 70,000 thoughts a day are negative and they allow them to take root in their mind. In such a state of mind, they are no longer inquisitive, they become narrow minded in their approach. So they are unwilling to learn and then they do nothing. They fail all four steps.

If you need more proof, think of the well known notion of 'beginner's luck'. What's that all about? Well let's think about it:

- What kind of thoughts do beginners have? Think of a person on her first day at work or of a person participating in a competition for the first time. What would they be like? They'd wash behind their ears; wear their Sunday best and would most likely have huge hopes for a great outcome. They'd be full of anticipation and excitement. So you can imagine what most of their 70,000 thoughts would comprise. *They are completely in the positive mindset zone. Nervous, but positive.*

- How 'hungry' are they to learn about anything that could be of assistance/ relevance to their project? Would they look up the new company? Maybe try and find their new colleagues on Facebook? Would they read about what happened in the competition in previous years? If, say, it was their first marathon would they look up as many facts and figures as possible about running a marathon? You bet they would. They would look it up, research it, ask friends and family and collate as much information as possible, consuming knowledge all the time. *They are learning.*

- Would they be tolerant about learning new things or would they be stuck in their ways? Of course the former, as there are no ways to be stuck in! It's a brand new experience. Everything is an option, everything is a possibility. They'd talk to anyone and would be happy to consider all manner of options. *They keep an open mind.*

- As 'beginners', by definition, they 'get on with it'. They make a start. *They act.*

Well that's the four steps ticked. No wonder these beginners are lucky so often.

In other words, luck is simply a state of mind.

So make sure you have the correct state of mind in place by thinking positively, learning, keeping an open mind and taking actions. Make sure you *decide* to be lucky, and the universe will conspire to make it happen.

You are living the dream. Good luck!

Chapter 2
You Mean Business

It's the end of the world as you know it

You have given it your all. Every bit of you and now it is chaos. You thought you were busy before, now you learn a new level of busyness; a level you didn't know existed. You are burning the candle at both ends. You feel that everything rests on you, and that's because it does. There's only you. If you don't ensure something happens, it won't. If you are a high flyer within a business, then the bucks stop with you as to whether your project works or not. All eyes are on you. If you are setting up a new business, you are completely on your own. In fact sometimes you feel quite lonely. Sometimes you are scared. 'What have I done?' you ask. Fear creeps back in. Was this a good idea? Why did I put everything on the line for this?

You know you have to start generating an income too. You feel added pressure. Freedom without the ability to make a living will not be sustainable, not if your livelihood relies on it. It then becomes a hobby. A hobby is where you do what you love, when you want, for however much or little as you want with no intention of making money in the process. If you can afford to pursue your passion without the need to make a living from it, that's absolutely brilliant. But if you have to make a living, perhaps even your family's livelihood depends on it, you will have to start making money at some point soon.

Then you are thrilled. You love your freedom. The passion for your project is growing by the minute. You start to see and feel the love from your groupies. You are on the receiving end of positive feedback and it keeps coming in. People say you are a breath of fresh air, they ask you where you were all this time and your competitors, (the frank ones), think 'why didn't I think of this?' It is exhilarating. And then you are tired. You are exhausted.

It's a roller coaster.

Then...You get a client, and another one and another because profits follow passion. I remember vividly going through this roller coaster experience myself. At 7.00-9.00 in the morning it was all about getting the children (then nine, six and a six month old baby) to school and the child minder. Then between 9.00-18.00 it was all about causing an epidemic and joining the revolution. I wrote the website content; I created the brand, the story, the Premise, the Ginger Business Plan, the Ginger Marketing Plan and the marketing strategies. I was meeting the accountant, and the IT support technician. I was learning all the compliance rules of the Solicitors Regulation Authority; I was dealing with the opening of the necessary bank accounts. I was winning clients. I had to make sure there were clean mugs and milk in the fridge to offer clients on arrival. I would run to the shop before the meeting, get the milk, wash the mugs and present the refreshments in the boardroom ready to serve. I would order the stationery. I would be out networking. I was writing legal tips for online magazines. I was buying office furniture. Then at 18.00 when the emails went quiet and the phone stopped ringing I would start the legal work often until midnight. Day in and day out. I hardly saw my children during the week.

I was exhausted.

I came downstairs one Friday morning sat on the kitchen chair and started crying, tears tumbling down my face, mumbling in between sobs 'I can't do this anymore'.

Growing pains
What a wonderful problem to have, to be the victim of your own success. But it is nevertheless a problem and it has to be solved.

At this point you need to pause.

Pause and ask yourself 'What was my dream?' 'What was my definition of success?' If, in my case, my dream was to leave my job, work as an independent lawyer three days a week and be at home with the children two days a week, then at that point I would have had to acknowledge that I had failed, albeit temporarily as this failure would have been simple to fix. I could have 'turned the volume down' even if that meant rejecting projects and jobs. Pretty quickly I would have been successful again.

But that wasn't my dream. My dream was to change the way in which business legal services were provided and purchased in the market place. So on that very teary Friday morning, I reminded myself of that. And the solution became immediately apparent. If I wanted to change the way in which business legal services were provided and purchased in the market place, I would not be able to achieve it on my own. It was just not possible. To achieve my dream I would have to grow a business and this entailed recruiting someone to help me. Simple. But then what raised its ugly head? Our old friend 'fear'.

But what if it all quietened down? How could I possibly take the risk of taking on someone, commit to paying them a salary when I had no idea of my workload further down the line? I had a handful of legal jobs on but once they were completed what then? What if the work dried up completely? What if there was insufficient work to keep both of us busy? As always, the fear was very reasonable. It made complete sense.

This is when you need to pause. Again.

Remember? Pause the bedlam in your mind, stare the fear in the eye and ask the one question: what's the worst that can happen?

Well the worst that could happen to me in this situation was that I would take on a new employee and after they had been with me for a few months there would be insufficient work for both of us. I reasoned that as long as I explained this to them from the outset, they could make an educated decision as to whether they wanted to join me or not. So I calculated what it would cost, looked at the number, (which wasn't insignificant for me) and asked myself 'Would I give up my dream for that amount?' I then asked other questions 'What if in fact it continues to be busy?' 'What if it gets even busier?' 'What's the best that can happen then?' If I didn't take on someone, I would never know.

Your first workmate

That teary Friday morning I made a decision. I was going to find my first workmate...

The following week I went to a networking event. I overheard a woman who I had met several times before on the networking scene asking another solicitor on our table if they were looking to recruit a law graduate as her friend was looking for a position. They were not, so I approached her afterwards. She explained that her friend had completed her law degree and law school successfully but had taken a five year break to have children and was now looking to go back into work on a part time basis. I was interested. It sounded like the perfect solution; someone with a background in law who could help me with legal research as well as everything else that needed doing. Because she was looking for a part time job payment would be pro rata. I might be able to afford her for longer if we didn't get busy quickly enough.

As I said, once you truly make a decision from the bottom of your heart, the universe conspires to make it happen. It did it again.

But back to this story, the one thing that concerned me was that the potential workmate was seeking a training contract. To qualify as a solicitor you have to work for two years as a trainee to gain practical experience. Finding a training contract is extremely difficult and many law graduates don't qualify as solicitors because they can't get one. So if I took her on for, say, six months as a trainee and it became apparent there was insufficient work for her I would have to let her go. This would reduce her chances even more of finding another training contract afterwards. I had to explain this to her from the outset.

We met a few days later and I was very impressed with her. She was smart, pleasant and seemed kind. I could really see us working together. I explained that Acumen was a brand new law firm. I shared my dreams and my plans but said that I couldn't promise it would work and that, therefore, it might be a good idea to have a six month trial period to see how things pan out. I also explained it was a 'hands on deck' job. No room for prima donnas. We would both have to wash up, buy the toilet paper, file, carry out admin jobs, engage in marketing activities and, of course, carry out legal work.

She loved the concept and we decided to give it a go. On the first day of April 2008, after seven months on my own, I recruited my first workmate.

This turned out to be an excellent decision.

Today, almost a decade later, we are still working together but now she is an experienced solicitor heading a department in the firm. The best that can happen, happened.

Chapter 3
They Are Not Your People

Colleagues
Once you have taken on your first workmate, you are now an employer. Various employment law provisions apply to you as well as the moral responsibility you have playing a big part in someone else's life. But it is their life. Just because you pay them a salary doesn't mean you have bought them between 9.00-5.00 or whatever hours they are contracted to work with you, not *for you*. You have purchased an arrangement and a set of expectations that go both ways. So many times people have told me 'I've met many of your people they are great' and I am always very grateful for their feedback as I know they mean well.

But they are not *my* people.

They are their own people with their own dreams and aspirations. Some are changemakers and FREE Entrepreneurs in their own right. They are my colleagues. My workmates. I set out my definition for FREE Entrepreneur earlier and as I explained it is not confined solely to people starting a business. I meet many people who work for themselves and I can tell you hand on heart they don't match the definition of entrepreneurs, definitely not that of FREE Entrepreneurs, as other changemakers I have met in other businesses as well as in Acumen.

The moment you stop viewing your colleagues as 'your people' or as people that work 'for you' is the moment you start to care about their dreams. Otherwise all you care about is that they facilitate *your* dream, not their own. It is of great benefit of course if your dreams and those of your colleagues are aligned. To work in harmony it helps tremendously if you all share similar core values and have dreams and passions that are aligned, but they are unlikely to be identical. We had three people who came on board who were not groupies; they didn't share our core values and it didn't work. So whilst it is important that your colleagues are groupies, they will have their own dreams and that's not a bad thing. Quite the opposite, it is a beautiful thing. Think of all the dreams that together you can help come true and in the act of doing so you will create something truly meaningful and powerful.

Let's go back to my first workmate for a moment. Due to her unique set of circumstances, her chances of finding employment would have been very limited: a woman (yes, I just said that), with young children (yes that too), who wanted to work part time (yes and that) and who had taken a five year break. I mentioned earlier how hard it was to get a training contract as it is. So what chance did she have in the black & white world? Virtually no chance. I realised this was a great opportunity to be ginger.

I saw her dream.

I saw her dream not to let her successful academic achievements go to waste. I saw her dream to remain a good and dedicated mother but a professional too. I saw her eagerness to go back into the world of employment. I knew then that she would give it her all. She would give it her all to make her dream come true. We all win when our dreams intersect. You could count on two hands how many days she had missed off work in almost a decade. She gave it her all, and she still does.

The word 'boss' puts a chill down my spine. I remember the local paper running an article with the title 'Acumen boss discusses her new plans'. I didn't like it. I am not a boss and I don't want to be one. A boss is someone who is in charge of workers or an organisation. I am not interested in either. Every team has to have a leader whose job is to inspire and help the whole team get to where it wants to go. But you don't have to boss people around.

Then when things go wrong, as they sometimes do, you know people have your back just as you have theirs. I had a close family member who had to be hospitalised for a lengthy period of time which meant I was away abroad for six consecutive weeks and all together for three months in one year. The business carried on working as usual and in that year we still managed to enjoy an increase in turnover and maintained our profitability.

When a member of staff was diagnosed with cancer we supported them all the way and paid them in full for their absence. When a member of staff who we thought was a colleague and a friend turned out to be the exact opposite and left us in the lurch, we all got together to work through the mayhem they left behind. It is when you have these relationships you know that you and your colleagues truly have your back and everyone else's. It is like family. And when things go wrong, everyone is there for each other. You don't even have to ask.

We are treated as we treat others; there is nothing new in saying this. But when it comes to colleagues, this simple rule is often overlooked. As Bill Gates said: "As we look ahead into the next century, leaders will be those who empower others", indeed, not those who boss others.

Empower others, but make sure you mean it. Give real power and everything, by definition, will become so much more powerful.

Chapter 4
Internal Innovation

nternal gingers
Once you have colleagues you have to start innovating internally.
The same reasons mentioned in Part II (In a World of Black & White, Be
Ginger), apply here.

After spending a considerable amount of time building a brand that is
innovative, different and mould breaking, if your colleagues return to
the office and the work place is run in a standard way, there will be a
misalignment. If you want your colleagues to 'go out there' and introduce
themselves as people who work in an innovative mould breaking company,
then the company has to behave in that way internally too.

As with external innovation, it doesn't necessarily have to mean
technological innovation or huge expense. It is first and foremost in your
mindset, attitude and approach. In our case, we innovated by scrapping
the internal hierarchy. We all make the coffee, answer calls and most of

the decisions are made by everyone in the firm. **ACUMEN** BUSINESS LAW is a democratically run firm, and everyone's opinion is heard and counts equally. This is an innovative approach in the general business world, let alone in the legal industry which is obsessed with hierarchy: Senior Partner, Junior Partner, Associate, Assistant and other such insignificant, waste of time disruptive labels. Some decisions such as salaries aren't discussed publicly because not everyone likes their finances discussed so we respect their privacy. But there aren't many other such examples. Most decisions, anything from which printer we should use to whether we should open another branch or not, are debated together in a weekly one hour meeting and agreed together.

Three motivators apply to all changemakers
There is endless research and books that discuss and show the clear link between an employee's motivation and the bottom line and that happy employees are the best sales people and company advocates. Whilst this is great, if that's your motivation for treating people well then the point is being missed.

If you want your workmates to be happy at work *only* because it will increase your bottom line, then it is still all about you. Caring for them is simply an outcome of caring about yourself. There is absolutely no problem caring about yourself (and so you should) and equally there are no issues with wanting to increase the bottom line of the business (you should certainly want that too), but if this is the sole or main motivator behind caring for your people it won't last as a long term strategy and you are back in the entreprewhores' zone.

You should care about your colleagues because you genuinely want them to have the best possible place to work; because you are genuinely concerned about their happiness *for their sake*, not yours. Because you acknowledge, accept and understand that they are people with aspirations and dreams, just like you. And if you care about them for their own good, you will create a happy work place for all of you and the increase in the bottom line will follow *as a result* not as the aim.

A major misconception in the business world is that employers think they can keep employees happy with their remuneration package alone. As we saw in Part I, when a person is deliberating whether to stay in their job or not, the salary consideration came fourth. The remuneration package is important, but it is only one factor and contrary to common belief it is not the most important one.

There are three motivators that apply to both business owners, changemakers and colleagues alike and, in my view, in the following order of priority:

(1) **Freedom** to make decisions and influence change
(2) **Sense of ownership** in the business they are working in
(3) **Financial remuneration** that is linked to success

Freedom is brought about by culture and values. For you and your colleagues to labour in freedom and create great and inspiring stuff, as per Einstein's quote in the opening of this Part IV, you must first and foremost embrace the concept of allowing freedom to make decisions and influence change wholeheartedly. Once you have done this you can bring freedom to your business by taking simple steps which will cost nothing. These can include:

- Encouraging ideas and initiatives by being inclusive, so everyone's opinion matters. This cannot be mere lip service.

- Recognising success in front of all. Every time someone, (including you!), does something positive, great, helpful, etc. let everyone in the office know. And I mean everyone. It doesn't matter how old or young we are, how senior or junior our position, we all without exception love being recognised for the good work that we do. At Acumen we have a regular item on the weekly agenda called 'Acusplendid' where we remind ourselves of all the positive stuff that happened in the last week. We also have a group email address that includes everyone as recipients which we use on a daily basis to acknowledge individual acusplendids.

- Scrap the blame/fault culture. You saw in Part II that this is part of our Premise. If someone has come up with an idea or initiative and it hasn't worked out, what do you think the consequences will be if that person is blamed? The opposite of freedom. They will feel trapped. They will no longer engage. You will shut them down. Blame and fault should not be confused with negligence. If one is negligent in what they do, e.g. they decide to take the day off knowing it is a trial day and they should be in court, this is negligence. But when things haven't worked out and when, with the benefit of hindsight, lessons can be learned, drop the blame and learn the lessons together.

- Have true respect for individuality. Truly and honestly understand, embrace and love the fact that we are all different. Have respect for it. Encourage individuality; it is the cornerstone for many ginger experiences.

- Be approachable, accessible and unpretentious. This is self explanatory and will be a natural outcome of dropping the hierarchy. Make sure you live the culture yourself.

Sense of ownership: you may want to consider sharing the equity in the company. There will be people in the organisation definitely worth considering giving shares to. These are the ones crucial to the success of the company now and in the future. I have been fortunate to experience this in Acumen.

But sense of ownership, just like freedom, is also achieved by culture and values and not just by the obvious ownership of shares. I know businesses where employees own shares but still don't act like owners.

Here's something a client told me years ago that really resonated with me: 'I want my employees to care that the light was turned off before they leave the office.' In other words, he wanted his colleagues to care about the business as much as he did. So many clients tell me they wish their colleagues cared like owners.

If your workmates are treated like owners, they are much more likely to care like ones. If you want them to care like you, treat them as you treat yourself. With the right mindset and culture you can make it happen.

Financial remuneration: where possible and if affordable try to pay people at market rate or above. There are times when paying less than market rate is appropriate or justifiable, for example when you train someone and in return you pay slightly below market rate, or where the payment structure is heavily led by a generous commission scheme.

If you have a bonus scheme in place, then make sure it provides remuneration that is linked to company success. Beside it being a fair commercial approach to financially remunerate, it also helps encourage a sense of ownership.

Chapter 5
It's None of Your Business

t's not *just* about you... or is it?

If you are planning to work on your own as a freelancer or on a one person project as a changemaker in a business, then naturally it is all about you. But if your definition of success is to grow the business or project beyond you, (even if these are speculative plans at this point in time), don't make it all about you. Don't call the business after your name, don't have all the systems and processes in your head, and don't centre it on you.

As the founder of the business or the changemaker within a business, you are likely to become the face of the business or the relevant project whether you like it or not. But that's not the same as making the entire business about you. Before setting up Acumen I read *"The E-Myth Revisited: Why Most Small Business Don't Work"* by Michael E. Gerber[20] which explains why you should set up your business with a franchise model in mind. As if you are definitely going to be replicating the business in the future and it will have to exist elsewhere without you.

I was very inspired by the book and this is precisely what I did when I set up Acumen. I remember even when I was still on my own, locating and centralising all the templates in a dedicated folder. I am not referring to legal templates, but to marketing, client care, systems and process templates. I remember at the time thinking I was going insane. There was no need for all of this, it was only me and I knew where everything was. But I always had my vision front of mind *to change the way in which business legal services are provided and purchased in the market place* and I knew I wouldn't stay on my own if I wanted to achieve this. It made life so much easier later on when everything was already centralised in one place. Of course these have been changed, improved, removed and amended over the years, but the basis was there from the outset.

So it may be your business, your project, your initiative, your set-up, but treat it from the outset as if it wasn't. This alone will help in focusing your thinking on growth and, as we know, thoughts become mindset which becomes habits which then become your reality.

If the reality you are seeking is that of a growing business with workmates, act like one from the outset.

Delegation
Many people find delegating extremely challenging. They have been doing it themselves, often very well, and the thought of letting someone else look after the baby horrifies them. Indeed I mentioned in Part I that your business or business project is your 'baby', your 'business bundle of joy'. But when 'the bundle' matures, you know it's time to begin the process of letting go. You gave it roots, but you know you must also give it wings to fly and be out there in the big wide world *without you*. It doesn't mean you stop caring, it means your baby is growing up.

Then, as the project/business grows you have to learn to let go, or in business terminology to delegate. It's not easy because *'no one likes my baby as much as me, surely'* but if you cannot or will not delegate, then your business will not grow. It is as simple as that. So, once more, you need to make a decision. If not growing is part of your vision, certainly don't delegate. But if it is, you will have to delegate as there is only one of you and there are only 24 hours in a day and neither of these factors are going to change. Not even if you are an online business because while your business offering may be automated, nevertheless there is a business with people behind the automation and, therefore, the same principles apply.

Fear of delegation is exactly that, fear. And as always with fear, as we discussed in detail before, ask yourself 'what's the worst that can happen?' and in this case more specifically, 'what's the worst that could happen if I delegated?' I bet it's not that bad. There may be inconvenience involved in finding the right person, financial expense, some time to be invested inducting and training and, even in the worst case scenario, if it didn't work, it may mean doing it all over again. But isn't it worth it so you and the person you are delegating to can follow your dreams? Look around you, so many people are doing it and if they can, so can you. If I can do it, I have no doubt you can too.

Then ask yourself 'what's the best that can happen if I delegate?' and see your dream materialising in front of your eyes. Isn't that worth it?

"Yesterday, thousands of people got married. Just about every one of these weddings went beautifully. Amazingly, you weren't there, on-site, making sure everything was perfect." (Seth Godin).[21]. It is possible that things will go really well without you. Sometimes you get a wonderful surprise and discover they go even better without you. That's a good thing! It means you are both doing a fantastic job as leaders and changemakers.

Delegation isn't about getting it done less well by someone else to free up your time, it is the exact opposite. It's about getting it done *better* by someone else.

Part V

Let's Get Operational

"Someone is sitting in the shade today because someone planted a tree a long time ago"
Warren Buffett

Chapter 1
Finance and IT

Stay strong

Passion, purpose, positive thinking and profits play a huge part in your business as we've seen. But so do the practical operational steps to ensure this all materialises. It is like buying a wonderful house but never maintaining it. It will resemble a dump in no time. Whether you are a business founder or a CEO, head of a division or engaged in any changemaking capacity within a business, you play a vital role in making sure the business stays strong. The business or project needs tidying, maintaining and looking after. This may seem mundane, less sexy or uninspiring, but without the important operational stuff, your business and indeed your project will start to fall apart.

Bad debt is truly bad!

I have a bee in my bonnet about bad debts! Bad debts should not exist and indeed they are bad! Very bad. A debt occurs when you have carried out work and you are not getting paid for it. If you invoiced in error, it is not a bad debt it is a mistake. You need to raise a credit note. If the debt is disputed and there is a legal argument, then you have various options which I discuss below.

But if it wasn't an error and it is not disputed, then it is a debt that must be paid. Businesses so very lightly agree to write off sums that are fairly due to them. Unless you are a charity or there are exceptional circumstances for doing this, writing off shouldn't be an option.

Make sure you have good systems and processes in place to chase debt. Have a system whereby if a payment is a day or more late it flags up and you can send a polite and friendly reminder. Then follow it up every single week until payment. The second follow up can also be a polite reminder as it may be that the relevant person was away, unwell or just had a very busy week. At this stage, you can give them the benefit of the doubt. The next chaser can be slightly sterner. Always remain polite, but you can ask more questions. The next one would be better done in person. Pick up the phone and have a good old fashioned conversation. Find out the problem (you can do that earlier if you want, but it might appear too keen if it's done a day after the due payment date).

If none of this works, the next stage can become more legal and the next one should be the final one before you refer it to your legal advisors to send a letter. At this stage you are nearly five or six weeks past the payment date. So if your payment terms are 30 days, it will be over two months since the date the invoice was raised. You should have been paid by now. You are not a bank and if you were, you would certainly have been paid by now with interest payments and charges too.

IT

Get expert IT advice, unless you are an IT consultant in which case you probably don't need to. Let them know your plans, what you need your business to do and seek advice on the best ways of using technology to help your business. Not rocket science, but so many of us try and do it ourselves and make a mess in the process.

Finance

If numbers aren't your forte get external help as soon as you are able. Over the years we have had two insolvency practitioners as members of the **ACUMEN** BUSINESS CLUB. I asked them both if they saw a common theme with businesses that failed and became insolvent. Whilst they both said it could be due to a multitude of reasons, they also said that nearly all of these businesses have one common problem whereby *'the people running the business had no idea what was happening with the numbers in their business.'* I am a lawyer not an accountant, so to make sure I always understand what is happening with the numbers from very early on I took on an FD initially on a freelance basis but later the position became a full time FD role.

Chapter 2
The 'Legals'

Sort it!

"*The most expensive mistake I ever made was taking a cheap lawyer*"... is something that was said to me by a new client at our first encounter...

So let's get the 'legals' right!

If your business needs a lawyer- you are doing well!

So many times when a lawyer meets new business people at networking events, on leaving they will say to the lawyer something along the lines of '*well you are very nice but in the nicest possible way, I really hope we don't need to meet again*'. They assume that if their business requires a lawyer they are in trouble. Either they are being threatened, chased or sued or they need to threaten, chase or sue others.

However, in the vast majority of incidents when you need a business lawyer, it actually means the opposite of being in trouble. It means your business is growing.

If you need a business lawyer, it means your business has grown so that you now need proper Terms & Conditions with your client; or you are employing people as part of your expansion and you therefore need employment contracts and a staff handbook; or as part of the increase in demand for your services/products, you have to collaborate with third parties so you need a freelance agreement or a joint venture agreement; or it is an indication that you are developing intellectual property which is becoming valuable and could provide you with income so you need a trademark or a licence agreement or other such protection for your IP.

By far, most of the services provided by business lawyers are required by growing and strong businesses. A business that hardly ever needs a lawyer is either not growing or changing, or they make that 'very expensive mistake' by saving on cost and dabbling with legal documents themselves.

So remember - if you have a business lawyer you are working with regularly, you are doing great!

Is there a cost effective way you can regularly work with your lawyer?

It is precisely because we know that growing businesses need to work with lawyers regularly and that it may not always be affordable that we set up the Acumen Legal Director Scheme whereby for a fixed and affordable monthly fee we are appointed as the in-house legal director in a client's business. Clients really enjoy working this way as they get the benefit of having a dedicated legal advisor without the expense of recruiting someone in-house.

Is there a way you can get such regular advice at affordable fees? It is worth looking into it rather than trying to cut on cost and risk exposure to legal liability?

Legal templates

I have a bigger bee in my bonnet about this topic!

Ok let's start by making one thing clear: all good lawyers subscribe to dedicated legal libraries that provide legal templates to work with. These legal libraries are not cheap but all good law firms make sure they make this investment because as I type these lines there is probably a law that is being revised or changed somewhere. Therefore to make sure that clients get the best service, good law firms subscribe to legal library services so all the legal documents are up to date and in line with legal changes.

However, our job as lawyers isn't to download a template and sell it on to you. If you want that kind of service, I am sure you can find plenty online for a nominal fee. Every business is different just like every situation is different. It requires great skill and legal know-how to make sure these templates are used to meet your very specific legal needs. I had a client who used one of these online Terms & Conditions which he adjusted himself to make sure they were tailored to his business. In other words, he was 'playing lawyer'. He then came across the following clause:

*"We **do not** exclude liability for any death or injury caused to you by our negligence."*

My client saw this and laughed to himself thinking it was a silly clause. Of course he'd want to exclude liability for any death or personal injury that may be caused to someone else. Why would he want to be liable? So he removed the word 'not' and his new clause read:

*"We **do** exclude liability for any death or injury caused to you by our negligence."*

However, removing the word 'not' rendered the entire agreement void as, in law, you cannot exclude liability for death or injury caused to someone else by your negligence and if you try and remove the liability via a contract, it will render the entire contract void.

This is just one anecdote to explain that templates alone are of no use whatsoever. In fact, they can be dangerous unless you have the legal knowledge to know how to apply them to your business. The cheap online templates that may be available are often provided by individuals who may not have the resources to ensure they are up to date and you have no idea what you are buying.

One client once 'saved' £450 on amendments that we suggested he should implement to his shareholders agreement and articles of association. Three years later when he sold his shares he lost £25,000 because these provisions were not there.

Similarly you can have a legal document that may give you an A in Law School but is not aligned with your culture and how you wish to do business. The lawyer therefore needs to apply business acumen as well as legal knowledge when preparing the documentation for you.

There are so many such examples, but I hope you get my drift. Don't save on your legals. Get it right from the outset; it will be worth it in the long term.

After all you have not come all this way for nothing. It is your precious baby, make sure you protect it.

The Business of Happiness

B ecause salaries and profits are measurable, we can count them and slot them into a spreadsheet. But what was happening before the revolution was that we were using the metric of salaries and profit as a tool for measuring things that were not meant to and, cannot be measured on a spreadsheet. Things like happiness.

Before the revolution we assumed that people who were richer were also happier. We created a Happiness Spreadsheet in our mind, whereby every time their fame and fortune went up, the Spreadsheet in our mind was updated and the level of how happy we thought they must be was rising in equal measure.

And then we wanted a Happiness Spreadsheet like that for ourselves. We wanted our Profit Spreadsheet to go up so our Happiness Spreadsheet would go up in parallel too. So we became entreprewhores. And as entreprewhores we embarked on the pursuit of money; of higher income, of more profit. We genuinely believed that once our pursuit was successful and we found 'more' money, whatever more meant to us, that we would be happier in equal measure.

But there is one thing that guarantees us **not** finding happiness, and that is the pursuit of happiness. Happiness isn't something that you can pursue and find externally, it is an outcome of a deep and meaningful experience within you. It is like hunger. You can't pursue hunger and find it externally. Hunger is an outcome of an experience within you, the experience of not eating.

Pursuing money isn't a deep and meaningful experience within you that leads to you finding happiness.

This isn't the same as saying that money will make you sad or that you should avoid it. Absolutely not. Have as much money as you like. Just don't expect happiness to arrive as a direct outcome of having money.

If you earn £50K instead of £25K, there is no happiness equation here. It doesn't automatically mean that you will be twice as happy. You might be ten times happier, you might be really miserable or your happiness level might not alter at all. You will no doubt have short term satisfaction of such increase, but don't confuse that with true long term happiness. Once your basic needs are met, your happiness does not correspond with every increase in your finances. The point is that your happiness level does not fluctuate in parallel to your financial fluctuation. Not in the long term.

You can't count happiness.

It is this profound understanding that formed the foundation of the Freedom Revolution with regard to business. Changemakers realised that happiness would not be found if they carried on climbing their corporate ladder constantly pursuing higher status so it would generate higher pay and nothing more; or if they set up their own business so they could constantly chase money, at all costs, and nothing more.

It was realised that happiness in business comes from a deeper and meaningful experience within the person in the business. It was finally understood that the pursuit of money to be happy in business is futile. It is irrelevant. And there was a coup.

There was a revolution.

In the revolution happiness comes about from the deep and meaningful experience of following your dream, passion and purpose. This brings about a true sense of freedom and it is this sense of freedom that generates the exhilarating feeling of true happiness. "...*when you are able to expose your work and your process to the right thing, to the metric that actually matters, good things happen*" (Seth Godin).[22] In the revolution we realised what actually mattered and then good things happened.

At **ACUMEN** BUSINESS LAW we scrapped the traditional annual appraisal forms and process, and replaced it with the Happiness Appraisal and it goes like this:

> "The main purpose of our happiness appraisal meeting is to find out about your dreams and see if we can make them happen. We all know that pay is a very important factor and we take care of this every year in the annual budget and bonus plans. But we all also know that it is not the *only* important factor.
>
> According to research, the aspect that matters to people the most at their work is to enjoy the work they do. Not salary (that came fourth), level of bonus, job title, status or benefits. It seems to be about **happiness**. So let's make the most of it!
>
> What's the best that can happen?"

Great stuff can happen and as mentioned in the first sentence of this book, whatever you are expecting it to be, it won't be that. It will be much better. But don't leave it too late. Please remember the discussion in Chapter 1 of Part II, it is not about your diary, it is about the momentum and about the now.

Remember, sometimes it is literally now or never.

This was realised by Steve Jobs, who has been quoted saying some incredibly powerful and moving words on his death bed. Here is an extract...

> "I have come to the pinnacle of success in business. In the eyes of others, my life has been the symbol of success. However... my wealth is simply a fact to which I am accustomed.
>
> At this time, lying on the hospital bed and remembering all my life, I realize that all the accolades and riches of which I was once so proud, have become insignificant with my imminent death.
>
> In the dark, when I look at green lights of the equipment for artificial respiration and feel the buzz of their mechanical sounds, I can feel the breath of my approaching death looming over me.
>
> Only now do I understand that... you have to pursue objectives that are not related to wealth.
>
> It should be something more important: For example, stories of love, art, dreams... stop pursuing wealth; it can only make a person into a twisted being, just like me.

...we can feel the love in the heart of each of us, and not illusions built by fame or money, like I made in my life, I cannot take them with me. I can only take with me the memories that were strengthened by love.

This is the true wealth that will follow you; will accompany you... will give strength and light to go ahead.

Love can travel thousands of miles and so life has no limits. Move to where you want to go. Strive to reach the goals you want to achieve. Everything is in your heart and in your hands."

Welcome to the FREEDOM REVOLUTION.

Ginger Scoring Sheet

Hello again!

This is the time we've all been waiting for!

Dig out your quiz answer sheet because you're about to find out just how ginger you are!

Unlike the Eurovision Song Contest, there are only ten scores to calculate so you will be done in no time!

Here are the scores:

1. When I am faced with fear, I:

    (a) Ignore it, trust my gut instinct and race ahead - **10 points**
    (b) Consult people I can trust, like family and friends, and then I make a decision - **50 points**
    (c) Consider worst and best case scenarios and make a decision accordingly - **100 points**

2. When one conceives the brand of their business or project, the first thing to think about is:

    (a) Make sure that my name and logo appeal to my target market - **50 points**
    (b) The reason for embarking on this business project in the first place- **100 points**
    (c) Name, logo, website, business cards, marketing collateral and brand colours - **10 points**

3. When I have an idea:

    (a) I first work out the practicalities and logistics to make sure it can be carried out - **10 points**
    (b) I mull it over at length to ensure it is the correct decision - **50 points**
    (c) If I instinctively think it's a great idea for business, I decide to do it first and work out the logistics later - **100 points**

4. When I embark on a new business or business project, I:

    (a) Go out there to meet as many people as I can to whom I could sell my products/services - **10 points**
    (b) Advertise (in magazines, radio, drop leaflets, etc.) to make as many people as possible aware of what I do - **50 points**
    (c) Look for opportunities to meet new contacts to tell them the story of my new project - **100 points**

5. Do you think outside the box?

    (a) What box? - **100 points**
    (b) No need to reinvent the wheel. There are tried and tested ways of doing things. The box is fine! - **50 points**
    (c) Easier said than done, it's not always practical - **10 points**

6. Do you have a 'dress down Friday' policy?

    (a) Yeah! It is always good to let your hair down at the end of the week - **50 points**
    (b) Every day is dress down Friday. As long as we look presentable when meeting customers, why should I care what I or anyone else wears while working? - **100 points**
    (c) No. To maintain our image and to ensure we are serious about our business, we dress to impress every day - **10 points**

7. Do you send regular newsletters to update your contacts on what you have been up to since the last newsletter:

    (a) Religiously! I think it is very important to inform our customers about all the great things we do - **10 points**
    (b) Sometimes. I think it is worth sharing when something special happens in the business - **50 points**
    (c) Never! Why would they want to regularly read about us? People don't have time to read stuff like that - **100 points**

8. How many activities a year does your business engage with, that are truly different to those of your competitors?

    (a) Four or more - **100 points**
    (b) Two or three - **50 points**
    (c) One or none - **10 points**

9. If I'm lucky, then:

    (a) I am successful by chance or I was simply at the right place at the right time - **50 points**
    (b) 'Lucky shmucky', there is no such thing as luck. Any success I have is thanks to me - **100 points**
    (c) Me lucky? Doesn't happen very often unfortunately... - **10 points**

10. If I need a business lawyer, it most likely means:

    (a) Oh boy... I'm in trouble! - **10 points**
    (b) It's going to cost me... - **50 points**
    (c) Good news! - **100 points**

900-1000 Points - Are you Prince Harry...? You are as ginger as can be! You have lovely fire coloured hair with lots of beautiful freckles. In a world of Black & White, you stand out like a gorgeous blossoming flower in an untidy garden. Keep up the good work!

500-890 Points - You are strawberry blond and you tend to get some freckles when the sun comes out. You have the right mindset and a great potential to be a real ginger. You have made an amazing start. Keep going. We believe in you!

Up to 490 points - You are dying your hair because you really want to be ginger. You are reading this book so I am predicting a transformation. I am sensing another ginger in the making joining the Freedom Revolution soon. We are waiting for you. We need you!

Do Share
Do you stand out in a World of Black & White? Inspire us and share your experience. What makes you ginger?

The Freedom Revolution community would love to hear your stories. Start a conversation now on Twitter **@Penina_Shepherd** or contact me via my website **www.penina.biz.**

APPENDIX

Your Legal MoT®

*"The leading rule for the lawyer, as for the man
of every calling, is diligence"*

Abraham Lincoln

Brief Introduction

I f I wasn't a lawyer I'd include a brief paragraph saying '*please do get legal advice to make sure all is in order and your business as well as you are legally protected*', but I am... So I couldn't help it and I felt I should include some legal tips for your business, as you are here anyway!

As I mentioned in Part I, in the first meeting we have with our clients at **ACUMEN** BUSINESS LAW, we carry out a Free Legal MoT® session either in the office if the client is local or via Legal FaceTime/Skype if they are not.

In this Appendix I will be carrying out a short Legal MoT® to help your business and I have included some case studies too.

Disclaimer: the legal position is correct at the time of typing these lines in early 2016, however the legal position may change subsequently but my crystal ball is charging at the moment and I can't tell if it will or what may change.

Another disclaimer (because that's how we roll): this should not and cannot constitute a substitute to you obtaining proper legal advice.

Penina's Perspective On...

If you are not in the mood for reading, not to worry I get it. Get some pop corn, put your feet up and go on the **ACUMEN** BUSINESS LAW YouTube Chanel and watch the series of 'Penina's Perspective On...' Each video is three to five minutes long and each has legal tips for your business.[23]

Or you could do both! This must be your lucky day. Let's get going, you know you want to!

Five 'Legal Circles'

The Legal MoT® comprises five legal circles. Whether you are a one woman band or you employ 5000 people, the same five legal circles apply to both of you. All businesses have the same five legal circles apply to them, the bigger the business, the more complex each circle, but nevertheless the same five circles apply to all.

Circle I
Your Business' Corporate Structure

Partnership
If you are a one person band it means that self employment is your corporate structure and there's nothing else you should do about it apart from contacting your accountant for tax advice. If more than one of you is running the business then, if you set up a limited company you are shareholders and in the absence of a limited company the default position is that you are partners operating in partnership.

If you are a partnership, then I recommend you enter into a Partnership Agreement otherwise you will be subject to the Partnership Act 1890 which, trust me, you don't want to be.

Limited company
If you operate via a limited company together with one or more other people, then I recommend you enter into a Shareholders Agreement

which is basically a business pre-nup agreement between you and your co-shareholder/s.

Imagine you and I started a business together as equal shareholders selling stress balls. It is all going very well and the business is doing great. We are both shareholders and directors in the business. We are both paid salaries as well as dividends. Then one Monday morning I come in and tell you that I have decided that selling stress balls isn't what I want to do anymore and that I want to be a poet. So I will be moving to a rural cottage in France and will concentrate on my poems.

I will work my notice and once I leave, you will no longer pay me my salary obviously. However, I still own 50% of our business; yes it is still our business. In the absence of a Shareholders Agreement to the contrary, whenever you declare dividends I will be entitled to 50% of them and when you come to sell the business, I will take a break from my poem writing and will pop in to collect my 50% of the proceeds.

> **Case study:** We had a client who was precisely in that situation. He came to see us as he was approached by a potential buyer offering him £5 million for the business but his departing shareholder who had not been involved in the business for nearly 3 years and with whom he had no shareholders agreement in place, was still entitled to £2.5million pounds.

A Shareholders Agreement will also deal with many other issues, for example:

- Can your co-shareholder/s employ an employee without consulting you?

- Can your co-shareholder/s buy a photocopier without consulting you? If the answer is yes, what about five photocopiers?

- Can your co-shareholder/s keep their shares if they leave? If not, can they sell them to their friend? If not, how do they realise the value for their shares?

- What happens if one of the shareholders becomes critically ill or dies?

As you can see, proper thinking needs to be carried out and the agreement must reflect how you want to implement them for your business. You can see why templates wouldn't work.

Circle II
The People in the Business

There are two types of 'people in the business': employees and freelancers.

Employees: With regard to employees, I will cover general employment law documentation as well as briefly discuss the topic of Employee Incentive Schemes, which is also my niche area of speciality.

Employment Law documentation: As far as your employees are concerned, it is very important that you have employment contracts and a staff handbook in place. The law doesn't actually stipulate that you need to have an employment contract; the requirement is to have 'written particulars'. But if you are going to sit down and write your particulars, then you might as well put together a properly drafted employment contract that is aligned with the needs of your business.

Your staff handbook comprises a list of policies that deal with a variety of issues such as disciplinary procedures, redundancies, maternity leave, paternity leave, use of the internet, work and pay during adverse weather conditions, social media at work, etc.

The staff handbook should not form part of your employment contract. You must remember that every contract can be changed as long as the other party to the contract agrees to the change and the agreement to change, and the change, is documented in writing. If you make your staff handbook part of your employment contract, then every time you want to amend a policy you will require the employees' consent and the policies of the staff handbook require more flexibility. It is therefore better not to make it part of the employment contract.

Similarly any bonus arrangements you may have with employees, should be a separate document and I always recommend making them annual. For the simple reason that one type of bonus scheme can work really well for one year but might not work that well in future years. If you do not make it part of the employment contract and keep it annual, it gives you the flexibility to review it every year to make sure you have the best arrangement in place year on year.

Employee Incentive Scheme: There are a number of employee incentive schemes to consider, but here I would like to briefly touch upon the Enterprise Management Incentive Scheme (**EMI**) which is by far the most popular scheme used by SMEs in England and Wales. The main reason companies opt for setting up an EMI is to reward, incentivise and encourage loyalty of the relevant employee/s by providing them with a sense of ownership and financial reward linked to company shares.

In very basic terms, the way the EMI works is that you grant employees (one or more) an option over shares in the company that they can exercise (i.e. become shareholders) on conditions that you set in the EMI Agreement. It is within the company's discretion to decide when and on what conditions the EMI options may be exercised, as long as they are exercised within ten years of the date of grant. For example, the exercise conditions can stipulate that the EMI option can be exercised after a fixed number of years; when certain performance conditions are met (e.g. personal targets, company's turnover, etc.); on the sale of the company; or on a number of these elements put together.

If the exercise is triggered by a sale of the company, then the employee doesn't in effect ever become a shareholder in the company as the employee will receive the cash in return for the shares on sale.

If the exercise is triggered by, say, performance conditions, then on exercise the employee will become a shareholder in the company. In this scenario you will need to decide if the shares that are subject to the options should have different rights to the other shares in the company. For example, would the EMI shares include the right to vote or to be paid dividends? You will also need to address the issue of employee shareholders leaving after exercise and what should happen to their shares then. There are a number of options available to you that an EMI legal expert should advise you on as it requires a technical analysis of the mechanism you want to put in place. The EMI option can be granted over a separate class of shares which means you can stipulate what rights will be attached to these shares.

The EMI is an HMRC scheme and offers the parties excellent tax benefits. If the option is not exercised within ten years for any reason whatsoever, including the employee leaving the company, then the scheme simply lapses as if it never existed.

Freelancers: There are two fundamental legal points you should know about freelancers. The first t is relevant to Intellectual Property (IP) and the second to their legal status.

Freelancers & IP: Imagine I am a well known designer and you came to see me to ask me to design your logo. Being so important and well known I demanded £30,000.00 (+VAT) for the work and for the full sum to be paid up front. Excited that your logo will be designed by famous me, you paid me the entire sum and I designed a blob for you as your logo. You were thrilled with it.

Who do you think owns the IP in the logo? Is it me (the designer in this case) or you (the person who commissioned me and paid me for the work)?

It is the designer.

If at any point in time you instruct a freelancer to make a design for you, draw your logo, set up your website, write content for you, carry out software coding, etc. it is the freelancer who owns the intellectual property rights in the work they have created and not you! It doesn't matter if you commissioned the freelancer or if you paid her a very high price for the work. The general principle of law is that the creator automatically owns the intellectual property rights in what they've created, subject to two exceptions to the rule:

(a)   if the creator is your employee; and/or
(b)   if the freelancer assigned the IP rights to you/your business in writing.

Make sure you get a Freelancer Agreement in place to protect your intellectual property, as well as many other important matters. A Freelancer Agreement is a mirror of an Employment Contract; the former is governed by general contract law whereas the latter is governed by employment law. So if you work with a freelancer on small matters, quite sporadically and on an ad hoc basis, then it maybe over the top to get them to sign up to a Freelancer Agreement and the best thing to do in this scenario is to get them to sign up to an Assignment Agreement that only deals with the IP assignment. But if you do work regularly with them, then make sure they sign up to a properly drafted Freelancer Agreement.

Freelancers and Legal Status: The fact that you decide that the person your business engages to provide services is a freelancer, does not make them a freelancer in law.

> **Case study:** A client of ours was a company specialising in fitting window blinds. They had a lady whom they offered to come on board as a part-time employee but she asked to be a freelancer. Her job was to visit your premises, measure the windows and provide a quote for the blinds which would be fitted by the company.

When the recession hit, the company informed the freelancer they would no longer be using her services because they would be taking the measurements themselves. The next thing to hit their desk was an unfair dismissal claim submitted to an employment tribunal.

When they came to see us, the first question they asked was 'What was she doing in an employment tribunal?' After all, they thought, she was not an employee and only employees can bring claims in an employment tribunal.

But was she not an employee?

To determine whether an individual who is engaged by your business is engaged as a freelancer or as an employee (regardless as to what contract you have entered into with them), the courts will carry out a number of tests, such as:

- Control - you would have more control over the working hours of your employee than of your freelancer.

- Tools - true freelancers will use their own tools whereas employees will be provided with the tools by you.

- Payment during absence - true freelancers do not get paid unless they turn up to work whereas employees can sometimes be paid even when they are absent e.g. holiday and sick pay.

- Integration into your business - the court will assess how integrated that person is with your business, for example if they are invited to your Christmas party. The more integrated they are in the business, the more of an indication it is that they are employees (but please read the caveat below).

- Are you their sole client or does the freelancer provide services to other clients? The former is more of an indication they are your employee and the latter that they operate as a true freelancer.

Caveat: the important point to emphasise is that the courts will look at all the tests together and not at each test in isolation. So if your freelancer joins you for your Christmas parties, that alone does not make her your employee. The courts will look at the true relationship with the individual; is it one of a client (you) and a service provider (freelancer) or that of an employer (you) and an employee?

Because if they are held to be an employee, then they are entitled to all the employment law rights such as minimum wage, holiday pay and more. Also HMRC will then demand all the Income Tax and national insurance contributions that will then fall due.

Circle III
Your Relationship with Third Parties

The most important third-party for every business is their clients. It is therefore of fundamental importance that you have proper Terms & Conditions of Business in place. What you must remember is that *every* interaction with your client whereby they buy your products or services, is a contract. If it was properly drafted, then you have a legally sound written agreement. If the transaction was agreed by text messages or emails, you still have a contract with your client but it is simply very badly drafted. If it was agreed verbally, then you still have a contract with your client but if there is an argument as to what it included then it is your word against theirs as there is no written evidence.

The two main differences between a properly drafted set of Terms & Conditions and the verbal or badly written agreements you have with your clients are that, firstly, if it is not written at all or written up badly your company may not come across as being very professional and, secondly, you are exposing your business to potentially serious liabilities.

Case study: Our clients, a building company had Terms & Conditions in place. A husband and wife booked their services for the entire summer months to renovate their house. Because of this, the builders rejected numerous new work queries, lined up subcontractors and started buying some of the materials. A day before they were supposed to start the work, the couple cancelled the job.

When they came to see us, it became apparent they had no cancellation provisions in place and the couple were not in breach when they terminated the agreement the day before. Also, both husband and wife were solicitors... This is just one example of how important it is to protect your business by having proper terms and conditions in place.

Every business will have something to protect that is really important to them. It could be cancellation provisions, intellectual property, secondment of your employees to make sure that clients don't poach them, payment arrangements, etc.

Other relationships with third parties that fall in this circle may be your suppliers, agents, franchisees, collaborators, referrers, etc. All such relationships will need to be legally protected in a properly drafted agreement that reflects the way you wish to work.

Circle IV
Your Property

'Property' in this context means physical property as well as intellectual property.

Physical property: if you're working from commercial premises such as an office, restaurant, workshop, etc. then you must have entered into a legal arrangement with the landlord. You may have entered into a licence or lease or you may have bought the freehold. It is fundamentally important to have these agreements looked over. Most leases can be negotiated when it comes to rent, break clauses dilapidation provisions, etc.

Intellectual property: Despite not knowing your business I can almost guarantee that its most important asset is your intellectual property. That is your name, logo, slogans, database, knowhow, software, client list, etc. In the olden days it used to be your premises, your machinery, but in this day and age it is nearly always your IP. So when you come to sell your business, what you will be selling is, in effect, your intellectual property.

Say your buyers instructed us to act for them on the purchase of your business for £4m. One of the first things we'd do is carry out due diligence on your business. This is so that we can report to your buyer on exactly what they are buying. For example, we may find out there is a £10m outstanding court claim against you, then our client, your buyer, will certainly want to know about this because once they buy your company it is they who will need to defend that claim.

But another important thing the due diligence will show is the legal position with regard to the ownership of the IP in your business. If it becomes apparent further to our due diligence that, actually, you used freelancers for your software coding but never entered into either a Freelancer Agreement or an Assignment Agreement with them then, as explained earlier, you don't actually own the IP in the software which might be the heart of your business and for which my client was about to pay you £4m. When we report back to our client we will explain that, legally, you don't actually own the IP in the software and the advice would be to either walk away or substantially reduce the purchase price. This will be the same position with regard to any of your IP such as name, logo, website, marketing collaterals, designs, etc. And, as I explained, it is your IP that you will most likely be selling so you must ensure you legally own it.

There are a number of ways to protect your intellectual property, the two most important ones are:

Trademarks: they are fundamentally important to protect your brand. You undoubtedly spend a lot of time, money and effort on promoting your brand and you should therefore protect it by registering a trademark. Relatively to other legal costs, trademarks are not expensive and are a really good way to make sure that you legally own your brand, including your business name, logo, slogan, etc.

A common misconception is to think that as you own your domain name or that you have a company name registered in Companies House, you don't need a trademark. However, anyone can set up a company called

'John Smith Limited' trading as 'your company name'. The only way you can stop them is by bringing an action of passing off against them which can be a complicated and expensive process and not always easy to prove and win.

Contracts: they are also a very good tool for protecting your IP. As you may remember I explained earlier that the general rule is that the creator automatically owns the intellectual property rights in what they've created, subject to two exceptions to the rule (a) if the creator is your employee; and/or (b) if the creator assigned the IP rights to you/your business in writing. We are concerned with (b) here. By having properly drafted contracts in place with sound IP provisions included, you substantially increase your chances of making sure you own the IP.

Circle V
Your Contentious Matters

Unfortunately it is very likely that your business will encounter contentious matters along the way. Those will either be debt recovery matters or litigation.

Debt Recovery: This is where you send a client an invoice and she simply doesn't pay. She might have said that the cheque was in the post; she was on holiday, was ill or simply ignores your payment requests. But the crucial point is that she doesn't dispute the fact that you are entitled to the payment.

A tip we provide our clients here is to send their 'final straw' email, copy in their lawyer at **ACUMEN** BUSINESS LAW and stipulate that if a payment is not made within, say, five working days, that they will have no option but to instruct their lawyer copied above to take over the matter. Then, if they still haven't paid, you can move on to the debt recovery stage whereby a solicitor's letter before action is sent to the client's debtor demanding payment for the unpaid invoice/s.

Litigation: This is where you invoiced the client requesting payment but the client is disputing the fact that you are actually entitled to the payment. For example, the client may be disputing the quality of your product/service that you sold/provided them or claiming certain rights that you are disputing (and vice versa). In such a case a 'merits of the case' assessment is required in order to ascertain the strength of your case, based on the agreement between you and other relevant evidence. The assessment of the case is then followed by legal advice as to the strength of your legal standing in relation to the specific matter so you can make an educated decision if you wish to pursue it further.

The idea is that if you take good care of the first four circles, the likelihood of becoming embroiled in protracted litigation matters in the fifth circle will be substantially reduced.

Saving on the cost involved in the first four legal circles, may lead to a very expensive fifth legal circle. I see it every single day in my work. Get professional advice to safeguard your business.

Because you and your business are worth it!

References

1. **Whatever You are Expecting it to Be, it Won't Be That**, Seth Godin, email-blog, 08 March 2016.

2. **Part I, Chapter 2**, The Vegan Society.
   https://www.vegansociety.com/about-us/key-facts

3. **Past I, Chapter 2**, PR Newswire, a UBM PLC Company.
   http://www.prnewswire.com/news-releases/global-organic-food-market-to-grow-at-over-16-by-2020-concludes-techsci-research-523104261.html

4. **Part I, Chapter 2**, Gustavo Tanaka, Brazilian author and entrepreneur.
   https://medium.com/the-global-future-of-work/there-is-something-extraordinary-happening-10492495c715#.tgfw96wen

5. **Part I, Chapter 2**, The Guardian, UK increased recycling rates fastest in Europe over past decade. http://www.theguardian.com/environment/2013/mar/19/uk-recycling-rates-europe

6. **Part I, Chapter 2**, Richard Branson's tweet, 18 May 2016.
   http://virg.in/ycqPM

7. **Part I, Chapter 2**, 'How Google Became Great'.
   http://www.evancarmichael.com/library/sergey-brin-larry-page/Searching-for-Success-How-Google-Became-Great.html

8. **Part I, Chapter 2**, 'Lessons Learned from Bill Gates', 'Sources of Insight'.
   http://sourcesofinsight.com/lessons-learned-from-bill-gates/

9. **Part I, Chapter 2**, 'Mark Zuckerberg on Passion, Cogzidel Technologies.
   https://blogs.cogzidel.com/2016/02/22/mark-zuckerberg-on-passion-startup-quote/

10. **Part I, Chapter 2**, 'The Purpose Economy', a book by Aaron Hurst.

11. **Part I, Chapter 2**, 'The Purpose Economy', a book by Aaron Hurst.

12. **Part I, Chapter 2**, 'The Purpose Economy', a book by Aaron Hurst.

13. **Part I, Chapter 3; Part Iv, Chapter 5**, Nelson Mandela's autobiography, quoted in Nelson Mandela Foundation- Living the legacy website, https://www.nelsonmandela.org/content/page/a-selection-of-nelson-mandela-quotes

14. **Part III, Chapter 1**, 'The E-Myth Revisited: Why Most Small Business Don't Work', Michael E. Gerber.

15. **Part III, Chapter 1**, 'Lessons Learned from Bill Gates', 'Sources of Insight'. http://sourcesofinsight.com/lessons-learned-from-bill-gates/

16. **Part III, Chapter 4**, Penina's Perspective On.. Series of 3-5 minute films on the **ACUMEN** BUSINESS LAW's YouTube Channel https://www.youtube.com/user/acumenbusinesslaw

17. **Part IV, Chapter 1**, The Robert Heinlein Interview and Other Heinleiniana By J. Neil Schulman, p.18.

18. **Part IV, Chapter 1**, NME on Paul McCartney and Kanye West http://www.nme.com/news/paul-mccartney/85552

19. **Part IV, Chapter 1**, Professor Philippe Gabilliet on Is Success a Matter of Luck?

20. **Part IV, Chapter 5**, 'The E-Myth Revisited: Why Most Small Business Don't Work', Michael E. Gerber.

21. **Part IV, Chapter 5**, Seth Godin 'All the events you weren't there to control' blog 02/04/16, http://sethgodin.typepad.com/seths_blog/2016/04/all-the-events-you-werent-there-to-control.html.

22. **The Business of Happiness**, Seth Godin '*Numbers (and the magic of measuring the right thing)*' blog 20/04/16, http://sethgodin.typepad.com/seths_blog/2016/04/numbers-and-the-magic-of-measuring-the-right-thing.html.

23. **Appendix- Your Legal Mot®**, Penina's Perspective On.. Series of 3-5 minute films on the ACUMEN BUSINESS LAW's YouTube Channel https://www.youtube.com/user/acumenbusinesslaw

Printed in Great Britain
by Amazon